Gaur Gopal Das has lived as a monk in an ashram in Mumbai for over twenty years. After years learning the antiquity of ancient philosophy and the modernity of contemporary psychology, he became a life coach to thousands in the city.

Gaur Gopal Das has been travelling the world since 2005, sharing his wisdom with corporate executives, universities and charities. In 2016, his global popularity exploded as he took his message online. With millions of views of his videos on social media, he has begun to lead a movement to help others achieve happiness and purpose in their lives and is now one of the most famous monks in the world.

THE WAY
OF THE
MONK

*The four steps to
peace, purpose and
lasting happiness*

GAUR GOPAL DAS

RIDER
LONDON · SYDNEY · AUCKLAND · JOHANNESBURG

1 3 5 7 9 10 8 6 4 2

Rider, an imprint of Ebury Publishing,
20 Vauxhall Bridge Road,
London SW1V 2SA

Rider is part of the Penguin Random House group of companies
whose addresses can be found at global.penguinrandomhouse.com

First published in Great Britain by Rider in 2019
First published as *Life's Amazing Secrets* in Penguin Ananda by
Penguin Random House India 2018

www.penguin.co.uk

A CIP catalogue record for this book is available from the British Library

ISBN 9781846046254

Typeset in 11.75/15.80 pt Adobe Caslon Pro
by Integra Software Services Pvt. Ltd, Pondicherry

Printed and bound in Great Britain by Clays Ltd, Elcograf S.p.A.

To my beloved mother, late father, grandmother and sister—
your love remains the foundation of all I try to do!

A word of caution: I have changed the names in this story. This adjustment is not only sensitive towards the couple whose secrets I am about to share, but also to avoid offending those who have ever fed me sambar that didn't live up to the standard set by the Iyers.

Contents

WHEEL 3: WORK LIFE

WHEEL 4: SOCIAL CONTRIBUTION

Preface

Have you ever experienced the Indian monsoon? It brings one of the fiercest, most thunderous downpours of water from the heavens. If you're caught in the heavy rain, it's nearly impossible to stay dry. Similarly, it is hard not to get caught up in the challenges and negative situations of the world. Feeling peaceful, happy and content is not about avoiding challenges in our life, but about how we navigate through these challenges to reach the type of life we want to live.

Aldous Huxley said, 'Experience is not what happens to a man, it is what a man does with what happens to him.' It's how we respond that makes all the difference. If there is one possession we have that is the most valuable and can truly transform our lives completely, it is our free will. We are the authors of our own life stories. Challenges and difficulties may fall upon us, just as the monsoon rains fall upon our head. We don't seek them or solicit them. They just come our way. We must choose how to respond.

Happiness does not come automatically. From a young age we receive methodical education in a variety of areas and fields, but happiness is usually not one of them. To live a happy life, with integrity and with balance, is one of life's amazing secrets which is revealed within this book. These are simple principles that can be used by anyone to experience a sense of satisfaction.

Do you ever feel irritable or frustrated? Do you ever feel that life isn't going your way? Do you ever feel that there is a key part of your life that needs attention? If the answer to any or all of these questions is a yes, it's a sign that your life is probably out of balance. The secret of life is finding balance: not too much, not too little. Just as a car balances on four wheels, we must balance the four crucial areas of our life: our personal life, our relationships, our work life and our social contribution.

Balance on an external level is about the alignment of the wheels. It is about adjusting our priorities based on the need of the moment, and focusing on that particular wheel which is out of alignment. At some points in our lives our work life may need more focus than our personal life. Have you ever wanted to spend time with someone who needs to meet a project deadline at work? It's impossible. They are too busy reaching their target. At other times our personal life may take precedence over everything else. Have you ever asked a couple organizing their wedding to spend more time at work? It's unreasonable to do so as they are planning one of the most important days of their lives. Dear friends, we must be willing to adjust our priorities to bring those wheels into alignment.

However, a deeper aspect of balance that resides within us is about our attitudes and values, which we explore in the different sections of this book. That attitude is like the air in the tyres of the car. If the tyres of the car are not at the correct pressure, there can be a puncture, stopping us from getting to our destination. This is why we have to navigate the internal aspects of balance. If the external tenets of balance are adjustment and alignment, then the internal ones are attitude and values.

As we balance ourselves externally and internally, it is fundamental to our success that we never let go of the steering wheel—our spirituality. If all the wheels are in proper alignment, if the air pressure in the tyres is optimal, but we do not have the steering wheel in our hands, we still will not be able to reach where we want to go. It was the Buddha who said, 'Just as a candle cannot burn without fire, we cannot live without a spiritual life.' Spirituality, in whatever genuine form of practice, brings purpose to our life and gives us a destination worth going to. At times we may feel empty or lost or have an existential crisis, when we feel that we do not know where our life is taking us. It is at those times that we must hold the steering wheel of spirituality tightly and press on. The steering wheel comprises four pieces: our spiritual practice (sadhana), the association that we keep (*sanga*), our character (*sadachar*) and our service to God and to others (*seva*). When all these aspects of the steering wheel are adhered to properly, they give us the ability to drive the car of our life towards its destination.

Let's get there, together.

ONE

Forgetting the Keys

As you become successful, do not forget the keys to happiness.

Although I grew up in Pune, my heart lies in a simple ashram, paradoxically situated amidst the skyline of downtown Mumbai. I have lived there as a monk for twenty-two years, during which time I have not only been studying ancient eastern wisdom for my enrichment, but also learning how to share its practical application with the world. People who attend my lectures regularly invite me to have lunch at their homes but, to their disappointment, I usually decline. As a monk, I have to be cautious of overindulgence; it is essential to stay regulated in our habits. But after months of pleading, I hesitantly accepted an invitation to go to Mr and Mrs home, a decision that would deepen my understanding of happiness in the long run.

Mumbai is notoriously humid in mid-May. It's the type of sticky humidity in which your sweat causes your shirt to stick to your back. But one only felt like that at sea level, not in the cloud-bound apartment of Hariprasad and Lalita Iyer situated in a high-rise in elegant Worli. This area of Mumbai is what Fifth Avenue is to New York, or Park Lane is to London. Indeed, if there were a version of the board game Monopoly for Mumbai, you would be paying a hefty price if you landed on Worli's distinguished towers: Palais Royale or Omkar 1973. And, here I was, a monk with hardly a rupee to my name, enjoying the cooling breeze from the Arabian Sea on the twenty-eighth-floor home of my gracious hosts.

The lunch started with me getting confused. I had never eaten sambar solely with a spoon, let alone three. They sat me at the head of their rich oak dining table, which overlooked the sea. A fragile, glittering centrepiece on the table illuminated the room as it shone in the midday sun. The table was set only for me—a weighty gold leaf-shaped plate with a satin napkin folded into a swan on it and cutlery of varying shapes and sizes around the plate—the three spoons lay in front of me, two knives to my right and four forks to my left. Four forks! I wasn't sure if we had four in our entire ashram as nearly everyone just uses their five fingers. I looked at Mr Iyer slightly uneasily and begged him and his wife to join me for lunch, not only to guide me through the maze of cutlery but to also give me company. It's no fun eating alone. Mr Iyer wanted to serve me lunch personally, but on my persuasion, he joined in. His wife, however, fought the offer and insisted that she would personally serve us both hot dosas and other preparations created by the army of chefs in their bustling kitchen.

And so—armed with a dessert knife in one hand and a salad fork in the other—I attempted to cut the dosa. It was clear this was an abnormal situation for me. Hariprasad smiled warmly at me, rolled up his sleeves and started eating with his hands, signalling to me that it was okay to do the same. I was delighted.

I have always believed that food tastes better when you eat with your hands. Although he was wealthy, Hariprasad didn't seem to have an air of arrogance around him.

'How are you so humble around so much prestige?' I asked him.

'I don't think I'm humble, but any humility you think I might have is due to my simple South Indian parents who raised me with so much love,' he replied.

Although there were many around his plate today, Hariprasad wasn't born with a silver spoon in his mouth. 'I grew up in a small village outside Chennai . . .' he began as he dipped his dosa in the sambar. Lalita came in with another round of dosas and sat momentarily, listening to her husband with interest. 'My father worked in a textile factory,' Hariprasad continued. 'His wages supported our family, and the factory gave us free cotton clothes that were passed down from my elder brothers and sisters. I'm the youngest, so most of my clothes had my brothers' names on the label. My father worked very hard for us.'

'But look at your clothes now! You can only afford them because you're the cleverest out of all your siblings,' Lalita interjected as she served him another hot dosa. They lovingly smiled at each other.

'What about your mother?' I asked.

'My mother stayed at home with us. She picked us up from school, cooked all our meals and was our counsellor when times were hard. Her hair was always tightly tied in a bun, but her arms were always open for a hug. She made our education her top priority because she wanted us to live a better life.'

'Well, it seems like you're living it now,' I said.

Hariprasad took no notice of my comment and continued, 'I remember the stress of both getting into IIT Bombay and then performing well there. It was worth it though because the Harvard MBA programme accepted me immediately, given that I secured a gold medal at IIT.'

'Are you talking about Harvard?' Lalita asked, while serving me two scoops of kulfi despite my protests. 'That's where we first met,' she told me. 'I was completing my medical studies there when we ran into each other at the Harvard India Student Group, and it was love at first sight. But I didn't meet the South Indian Hariprasad then, I met "Harry", as his American friends called him.'

'Well, I'll call him Harry from now on!' I laughed.

As lunch came to a close, Harry spoke of the work he does as the director of a multinational consulting firm. Harry's success at Harvard gave him a boost—thirty-five, he was already one of the youngest directors in the company's history and he was responsible for the firm's Asia operations.

'We both are trying to help as many people as possible before we think about children. We want to empower people to be successful,' Harry said, holding his wife's hand.

I was pleasantly surprised at how cultured and courteous this couple was. Lalita's world-class sambar also symbolized the warmth and love between them.

'Thank you for a wonderful lunch!' I said to them, signalling that I had to leave. 'I would love to stay longer, but we have meetings at the ashram in an hour. Can you call me a cab?' I requested.

'A cab!' Harry exclaimed as if offended. 'Please let me drop you back. The ashram is only thirty minutes away.'

I thanked Lalita for the delicious meal. She thanked me back with a smile, but I noticed that she was holding her stomach as though she was not feeling well.

I thought nothing of it and neither did Harry. We rushed to the elevator, which transported us from the clouds into the underground garage in moments.

Harry frisked himself in a panic as the elevator doors opened. It was the same expression one has when they cannot feel their phone in their pocket. 'I've forgotten my keys,' he said, as he vigorously pressed the button for the elevator to take him back to the twenty-eighth floor. 'I'll be right back.' He left me in what seemed like a deserted parking garage.

As we hurried to his car, I expressed how deeply impressed I was that a couple of their stature, their wealth and influence was reconnecting with their spiritual roots again.

'Can I tell you a story that I think you'll appreciate?'

Harry nodded as we both settled in for our short journey across town. He turned on the passenger light and gazed at me intently as I began speaking.

'Going on a holiday with your friends is one of the best experiences you can have. Before I became a monk, three of my close friends from university in Pune and I decided to take a trip to New Delhi together. We had booked a hotel but little did we realize that our room was on the eighteenth floor of a high-rise building,' I said, watching Harry reverse the car from his parking spot. 'After we dropped our bags off, we decided to explore the city by autorickshaw. We started at Red Fort, ate lunch at Chandni Chowk, meditated at the

Lotus Temple and then rested on the lawns around India Gate. It had been a good day. Tired and slightly hungry, we decided to return to our hotel and order room service. We arrived at the hotel just after sunset, to the news that the elevator had broken down.'

Harry gasped. 'What did you do?'

'We were young, so we decided to walk up all the way to our room.'

'We were exhausted by the end of it, but as the saying goes, time flies when you're having fun. Speaking and laughing with friends makes everything easier.'

'I agree,' he said, nodding. 'What did you all talk about?'

'Well, we told jokes and stories, made each other laugh, mocked each other. We moved from floor to floor with no complaints whatsoever. On the fifteenth floor, we realized that one of our slightly chubby friends wasn't saying much. "Are you okay?" I asked. "I'm fine," he said bluntly. We all have that one friend who is terrible at telling funny stories. He was that guy.'

'All my friends are funny!' Harry exclaimed.

'Well, you're probably the unfunny one then,' I teased. 'So after a few minutes of persuasion, we convinced this friend of ours to tell us a story. He stuttered at first, but then blurted out, "My funny story is that I've forgotten the keys to our room in the rickshaw." Our faces dropped. We had just learnt about the principle of ahimsa, or non-violence, at the Lotus Temple, but in that situation, ahimsa was impossible to practise! Using all our power of restraint, we started our silent journey back down to the reception, praying that the hotel had some spare keys.'

Harry burst out laughing. 'I can imagine the anguish on your face when you found out he didn't have the key.'

I nodded. 'However, only years later did I understand the lesson behind this story. I thought of it again today when you forgot your car keys. Harry, you have made incredible progress in life. People only dream of the kind of success you have achieved. From studying at prestigious institutions around the world to having a loving partner, living on the top floor of a skyscraper, having a seven-figure salary and a professional reputation years ahead of your age, you have come a long way. However, I am so glad that you haven't forgotten the keys to your happiness as you have moved up on the ladder of success. As a society, it's all too easy to focus on our external achievements and forget to assess whether we are happy with the state of our life. I'm relieved that you haven't neglected that aspect of your life.'

'I suppose so . . .' Harry remarked uneasily. He wasn't smiling any more. I sensed the change of tone in his voice. An awkward silence fell upon us as we left the underground parking.

There was something he wanted to say, but I didn't know what.

TWO

Seeing beyond the Obvious

Behind the smiles, everyone is going through personal struggles we know nothing about.

Have you ever walked into a room where two people have argued? You can immediately sense the stale energy in the room; the silence between them can be deafening. Miscommunication can spark similar tension. When Harry fell silent I found myself wondering: Had I said something wrong? Had I offended him? Insulting someone who has hosted you at their home is one of the most regrettable things one can do. Two minutes passed before I decided to break the deadlock.

'So where did you buy this car?' I asked, trying to change the subject to something more palatable.

Harry seemed to appreciate that I was trying to find common ground and followed suit. He still didn't seem to feel comfortable sharing with me whatever it was he was thinking. 'Well, I needed to buy a car after I sold the Mercedes. My wife and I were taking cabs everywhere for the first few weeks. One day when we were visiting some friends in Juhu, the cab stopped at a traffic light directly outside the Lexus showroom. That was when I saw her—sparkling from within the polished glass. It was love at first sight!' He cheered up at that memory.

'This car seems like your prized possession,' I replied.

He nodded repeatedly. 'There are not many things in the world that can make you happier than a car like this.' Harry slammed the brakes, our seat belts tightened, and I saw him firmly gripping the steering wheel. We came to a sudden halt. Carried away by his thoughts, he had not realized that the traffic had built up ahead. 'Sorry about that, I wonder what the problem is,' he said apologetically, peering ahead.

'No problem,' I replied. 'Are you okay?' I asked, a little startled.

Harry gazed into the distance, trying to see the root of the problem, but had no luck. 'Yes I am okay, but I'm surprised. There is never traffic here!' he said, sounding disappointed.

Although things have improved to some extent, Mumbai is still known as India's 'crash capital'. It has roughly the same number of cars as London, but more than four times the number of road fatalities. Cars can sometimes be reckless as they zip past red lights and try everything to zigzag through dense traffic jams.

However, for the moment we were trapped in his Lexus and not going anywhere. I messaged one of my colleagues that I would be late for the meeting. 'We're stuck!' I uttered, trying my best to be heard over the din of cars consistently honking with no results.

'Even in my new car, I'm stuck. It doesn't matter how fast it can go. I'm stuck!' Harry's voice choked up. 'Why do I feel so STUCK?' he screamed as he hit the steering wheel of his prized possession. 'Is it the fault of the people in the cars ahead of me? They caused the traffic? Is it that they didn't build the roads wide enough? I didn't build the roads. Or is it my fault?' His voice trembled. 'Did I buy the wrong car? Should I have bought a motorbike? Is it too late to buy a motorbike?' I sensed that something was going on in his life that he wasn't telling me about. I put my hand on his shoulder. His head dropped, and he placed his hands in his lap. His lip quivered, and he looked away from me, out of the window. In the reflection of the driver's side window, I saw a few lonely tears leave his sorrowful eyes. 'I'm sorry,' he said. 'I don't know what came over me.'

'Don't be sorry. We can all feel stuck at times. Why do you feel stuck?' I asked empathetically.

'I'm sure you don't have time for all of this.'

'I have all the time in the world for you. Firstly because we're going to be stuck here for a long time, and secondly because you have fed me the best sambar I've ever tasted in my life!'

He chuckled as he dried his eyes with his silk hand-kerchief. He knew I was trying to lighten his mood. When we comfort someone, it is easy to fall into their sorrowful energy, which can perpetuate their suffering. It's important that we bring positive, non-judgemental energy into these conversations.

'Where do I start?'

'Wherever you feel comfortable,' I whispered. 'I'm listening.'

He sighed and then began. 'Only a fool would say that he is not happy while driving a Lexus, but then I guess I am that fool. I have everything that I could have dreamt of, but within myself, I have this sense that something is missing.'

He looked out of his window again as if gazing into the lost past that he was about to reveal to me.

'It started at IIT Bombay. I never wanted to go there in the first place. I never wanted to study engineering, but my parents wouldn't take no for an answer. They insisted that "engineering is where the money is. If you get into IIT, life will be yours." If I ever questioned them, they would make me feel guilty by bringing up how much they did for me and how I shouldn't let them down.' He paused, as he thought the traffic was moving. It was a false alarm; we were still stuck. He continued, 'I think my parents were living their ambitions through me. My father was fascinated by the updating software in the textile equipment at his factory. He wanted me to be one of those superheroes at his factory who could come in and solve any technical problem.'

'You may not be a software engineer, but you seem to be doing well now. Aren't you?' I pondered. 'You went to Harvard!'

'Harvard was me rebelling!' Harry snapped. He took a deep breath. 'I had to get away from my parents and siblings. I wanted to live my own life, so I escaped to America. I know it seems ludicrous, but I didn't think about the Harvard MBA programme thoroughly. I just took it without thinking, just to get away. I had a full scholarship. After years of studying the wrong thing, I wanted to live my own life.'

'So was Harvard the solution?'

'Unfortunately, no. I completed the course, but it wasn't my calling. One great thing was that I did meet Lalita, or

Lily, as her friends would call her there. Both of us being South Indians, we instantly connected. Forget this car, that was surely love at first sight! I was also fascinated that she studied medicine and wanted to be a paediatrician. Maybe I was slightly jealous of her at times because it was there that I realized I wanted to do medicine too. But it was too late. I didn't have the time or the money to study medicine. So I kept it all in, and we returned to India for our marriage.' It was taking a lot out of him to reveal all of this, but I did not want to interrupt.

'Our marriage is amazing. Well, it started amazingly. Lalita was training to be a doctor for children, and I was headhunted for a job at my current consulting firm. They promised me a six-figure salary, not including my bonus. I've come up the ranks rather quickly. But at what cost, I constantly ask myself. The stress and long hours of both our jobs has weakened our relationship. We have little time for each other, let alone time to raise children. The sweet words Lalita briefly spoke to me at our home are rare. She has no idea how cutting her harsh words are to me, which leads to fights and, well, you know, marriage problems. It got so heated the other day that she yelled she wanted to get a divorce,' he said, looking out of the window again. The sea, which had earlier given us its cooling breeze in his apartment, was now shimmering and sweltering. 'How can love that started so pure evaporate so quickly? Funnily, despite all this, I'm at a stage where I do not like my work, and I don't look forward to being at home. But with my status, who will believe that I'm not happy?'

He certainly was *honest*, I thought to myself. Our egos are such that admitting our sorrows to someone else comes when we are incredibly humble or when we are in considerable pain. I felt he was a mix of the two. We tend to take everyone at face value, equating what they have on the outside to how they feel on the inside. The paradox of our times is that those who have the most can often be the least satisfied. We have mastered how to look successful, but not how to organize our lives so that we feel successful. These were the thoughts that came to my mind when he was speaking, but I kept them to myself. To me listening to understand is more important than listening to reply. The wheels of the car edged forward a few metres. At least we were on the move.

THREE

The Journey Begins

*Having a friend to listen to your problems and discuss them
with you is the beginning of finding a solution.*

What do we do when people we are close to are sharing their
worries with us? I wanted to say so much as Harry spoke
of his inner turmoil, but then I remembered my training as
a monk: Our silent presence can be more powerful than a
million empty words. We all have two ears and one mouth;
the amount we listen and the amount we speak should be done
proportionately. Rarely do people want an active solution to
their problems before they have been thoroughly heard and
understood.

I remember the early days when people used to come
and confide in me. I was a young, eager, fresh-faced monk
then, keen to save the world with my newfound sense of
purpose. In my immaturity, I would pounce on the solution
as soon as it came to me, not understanding that people
don't care what you know unless they know you care. In
fact, the answer to all problems related to the human
condition seldom excludes a conscious, compassionate ear.

The attitude of listening attentively is equally essential to the solutions we may present. I was not going to make that mistake this time with Harry.

I was glad that the traffic was clearing up, and so were my thoughts. A few moments of silence passed before I spoke. 'Harry, I'm so sorry you're going through this. Thank you for trusting me and sharing this. Even when you just speak to someone about your problems, do you not feel lighter? Do you not feel hope that things will get better?'

Harry looked at me, unconvinced. 'I want to get out of this mess. But I don't see a way out without ruining my life completely. I'm nearly forty years old; it's too late to make any dramatic changes. What should I do?'

What should I do are the four words any life coach hates, I thought. This is because any direct advice given by them turns into a 'magic spell' that if followed will provide 'guaranteed results' because Gaur Gopal Das said so. But that is not the case. Following blindly like sheep can lead us astray. Making choices in life is like buying something at a shopping mall. The sales assistant may show us all the products available, telling us the pros and cons of each of them, but we must make the choice in the end. The final decision is our responsibility.

'I'm not your guru, I'm your friend,' I asserted. 'We must make our own decisions, and I can only help you within my capacity. I do not know it all, nor do I claim to, but from my experience of being a friend to thousands of people around the world, you are not alone. Many people are going through similar struggles to you.' Harry sighed again, but it seemed like a sigh of relief, as we crept through the Mumbai traffic.

'Do you see how many people are stuck in this traffic jam?' I asked. 'They are all like us. They may be in different cars, but they are all stuck.' We all have three things in common: we are all stuck, we all have a journey to complete and we all have a destination. Now imagine the traffic jam all cleared up. We would all be free to complete our journeys in peace and reach the destination that we choose.'

'What's that got to do with my situation though?' Harry retorted.

'There is a traffic jam within our minds, Harry. And that traffic jam is stopping each one of us from reaching our true potential. Imagine if we knew how to clear this disruption. No fumes of insecurity causing us to cough, no one honking at us, distracting us from what's important, and plenty of fuel to sustain us so that we can live a life worth living.'

There were no tears in Harry's eyes; I could only detect interest.

'The process to clear the traffic within my mind started twenty-two years ago. I regret the pain I caused my parents, but at that time I ran away from home to become a monk. It was then that I learnt about the wheels of life. All of these cars around you have four wheels equally weighing down on the axle. The loss of air in any one of these wheels can slow you down in reaching your destination; the loss of one can be fatal. Therefore, it's imperative that your wheels are regularly checked and maintained. Similarly, there are four principles that form the foundation of a happy life. They aren't based on any label we place on ourselves and apply to all, whether we're monks or married, young or old, rich or poor, atheist or religious. They are not dependent on nationality, race, gender or profession either.'

Harry looked me straight in the eyes as the car halted again in traffic. 'I'm ready to learn them. In fact, I've been ready since I was eighteen.'

WHEEL 1
PERSONAL LIFE

FOUR

Growing through Gratitude

We must find positivity in the bleakest situations and live by the principle of gratitude.

Harry's fair complexion brought out the contrast in his dark-brown eyes. *The eyes are the window to the soul*, I thought. As he stared at me, I noticed parts of his sclera were bloodshot, partly from the stress of telling me his miseries and partly from the excitement of the conversation that lay ahead of us.

'The traffic of the mind, you were saying . . .' Harry said, eager to get back on track again. We lost eye contact briefly as he stretched his neck above the steering wheel to see if the traffic was clearing ahead. It was, albeit at a sluggish pace. 'So, the traffic of the mind,' he repeated.

'The traffic of the mind.' I smiled at him. 'The mind is what we use to perceive the world. We don't see things as they are, we see things as we are. Like your sunglasses . . .' I pointed to his designer glasses resting on the dashboard. 'When you wear them, the way you see the world changes. Things that once looked bright now look dull and lifeless. The things themselves haven't changed. Our perception has.'

The car at a complete standstill, Harry fiddled with the frames of his sunglasses, pondering my point.

'But things do change over time. My wife and I have become entirely different people.'

'I agree. The sands of time slow for no man. Things change for better and for worse, but what we choose to perceive is up to us. And that is a personal choice. Do we see the positive or the negative in a situation?'

I could sense his confusion.

'Let me give you a personal example,' I said and explained.

See the Positive

We all boil at different degrees. Some of us have temperaments like the Indian summer—hot, sticky and easily irritable. Yet some can remain level-headed in the worst of calamities, and as a monk, I was taught to control my emotions. So naturally, I assumed that I was in the latter level-headed category. That was until the day I realized I wasn't there yet.

To most people, the word ashram induces a romanticized vision of a temple situated in the foothills of a mountain whose name is difficult to pronounce. But not our ashram! Our ashram is a network of corridors in South Mumbai, a part of town that never sleeps. With over 100 monks living together, it can feel congested at times. One can imagine how long we're waiting for the bathrooms in the morning.

One day, ten years ago, I stormed into the room of my spiritual guide, Radhanath Swami. We're fortunate that he lives with us in the ashram, giving us easy access to him to share our joys and listen to our grievances. Have you been inside his quarters? They're extraordinary! If you could capture the smell of simplicity and sell it as a fragrance, it would be the essence of his room. Measuring a mere 5 sq. metres, with two simple tube lights and straw mats that line the floor, it feels as if one is entering a village home. The place is barren of furniture except for a small table that rests a few inches above the ground and a wooden chair for the elderly guests who visit him. Bookshelves line two of the walls up to the ceiling, with ancient books of wisdom sitting side-by-side with contemporary research. Musical instruments—a harmonium, and a mridangam drum—sit next to the focal point of the room, a small altar on which rest the deities of his meditation.

'It's all changing,' I whispered under my breath as I knocked on my guru's door.

'Come in!' he said. I sulked through the wooden doors with my head down. Radhanath Swami was sitting on the floor at his modest desk, his legs crossed and back straight. I repeated what I had said a little louder as I sat down and crossed my legs.

'It's all changing!' I couldn't take it; I had to tell him.

'Gaur Gopal?' he said inquisitively in his American accent that now had hints of an Indian one. He peered at me over his reading glasses with a penetrating gaze. He closed the book he was reading, which had a cover that looked like a relic from a bygone era, and went back to his original stance with his hands in his lap. I had his attention. That was my signal to speak.

I exploded. For forty-five minutes I nitpicked every grievance I had with the management of the temple and the many people who had wronged me. I complained that if this continued, it would ruin our community. I felt like a self-appointed saviour who had to point out these negative mannerisms creeping into our society. 'If we do nothing about all this, everything will be spoiled,' I finally ended. He sat there with a grave look on his face. Not a word left his mouth as I grumbled on.

'Have you finished?' he said sternly.

I sighed. 'Yes.'

'There are so many positive things happening in our community,' he started. For the next forty-five minutes, he did not mention a single complaint I had made. He only focused on the positives, uplifting my mood. 'I am not saying these problems don't exist, but the real problem is that when negativity consumes the mind, not only do we lose the vision to see the beautiful things around us, but also the ability to solve the problems that confront us. We have to train our mind to focus on the positive and feel empowered to deal with the negative.'

He then spent equal amounts of time going through the practical solutions to all my problems and then swiftly instructed me to go for lunch with all the other monks in the dining hall. He did not ignore the fact that some of my complaints were genuine.

It was not that the problems I had were not real. We all go through real challenges, for which solutions should be found. But what Radhanath Swami taught me was the power of having a positive state of mind while dealing with problems constructively.

'That brings a lot of clarity,' Harry said.

I could sense a 'but'.

'But how long did your positive attitude last? Are you telling me that Radhanath Swami just told you to be positive and it miraculously happened?'

'Well the miracle lasted at least an hour until lunchtime.' I laughed. 'This state of mind develops over time, and I realized that fully while eating lunch.'

The Cumin Seed

I left Radhanath Swami's room in high spirits. That's one of the effects of enlightened people: they make others feel inspired in their company. I galloped to the lunch hall (not literally; anyone who has ever worn a dhoti would understand how hard that is) elated and full of positive energy. The kitchen at our ashram cooks lunch for over 200 people daily. They have pots bigger than some grown men, and gas burners with flames larger than many ceremonial wedding fires.

Steamed rice, dal (lentils), spicy vegetable curries and hot flatbread chapattis—a simple, but satisfying lunch. What enhanced the flavour for me even more was the new appreciation for the people around me. The people in the room were a bit like my lunch. On occasions, the dal does not have enough salt, the curry is too spicy, or the gulab jamun has a bit too much ghee. However, they still nourish me. I looked at every face in that hall. I may have perceived faults in them in the past, but they had all helped me in my journey. I learnt on that day that when we think negatively of people, we should immediately counteract that energy by contemplating three positive qualities they have. I did make some awkward lingering eye contact with many of the monks in that hall as

I gawked at them, leaving them with confused expressions. But my intention was correct; I was training the mind to see the good.

As I digested my thoughts and lunch, I returned to my room to plan for a lecture that I was giving that night. I opened my laptop, which revealed a hoard of unread emails. I did not have time to read them considering my pressing evening deadline. *What to speak about?* I thought as I rhythmically tapped my fingers against the side of the laptop and rocked in my chair. Nothing came to my mind.

I was preoccupied with something in my teeth. A small cumin seed had lodged itself between the lower molar teeth on the right side of my mouth. I relentlessly fiddled with it. It was as if my tongue was playing tennis against my teeth, with the seed as the ball. After fifteen minutes of frustration, and feeling as if I was two sets down in this heated game, I went to the bathroom. My first tactic was rinsing my mouth with water. I used a range of motions to flush out the cumin seed, but I had no luck. The spice that had usurped the space between my teeth stayed put.

My second tactic increased the pressure on my unwelcome friend: dental floss. To be honest, and I want to apologize to any dentists reading, I rarely flossed so I did not have the manual dexterity to use the minty-fresh string. My last port of call was my interdental brushes that I used occasionally. They are little fine-bristled brushes that fit between the teeth and look like tiny plaque-fight swords. As you can guess, I was successful. With one delicate swoop in between my teeth, I stabbed the cumin seed straight in its core, banishing it from my mouth forever. It was a small, but significant victory.

Returning to my laptop, I knew precisely what I would present that evening: my experiences with 'Radhanath Swami and The Cumin Seed.' It was a sufficiently intriguing, but ridiculous, title to entertain the crowd. However, my incident with the seed had a valuable lesson.

The mind is like the tongue. It drifts towards the negative areas of our life, making us restless and uneasy. It schemes to uproot the problems that are causing us so much pain, not realizing that the persistent scheming is causing us more emotional damage. The mind neglects the thirty-one other 'seed-free' areas of life, choosing not to focus on the simple joys available to us. This is not to say we shouldn't deal with problems in our life. We need practical solutions too—interdental brushes are necessary. But we should not be consumed by them; that leads to misery. We have to focus on gratitude.

Gratitude is not a feeling; it is a state of mind that can be developed, and it allows us to tap into a reservoir of unlimited positive energy. Being grateful happens in two steps. The first is to realize that there is good in the world and that good has fallen upon us. The second is to know that goodness is coming from something other than us, that an external reality is giving the gifts of grace to our very own reality. This could be our family, our friends, nature and even God. We have so much to be grateful for!

Statistically, we always have more to be grateful for than ungrateful. Ingratitude means to forget the blessings in our life, to ignore the kind things people have done for us. It is not just positivity we feel when we embrace gratitude. Better sleep, the ability to express more kindness, feeling more alive and even having a stronger immune system are all benefits of being thankful.

A poem composed by Johnson Oatman, Jr, which we had sung in our primary school, summarizes my message eloquently:

> *When upon life's billows you are tempest-tossed,*
> *When you are discouraged, thinking all is lost,*
> *Count your many blessings, name them one by one,*
> *And it will surprise you what the Lord has done.*

'So gratitude is the key to remaining positive and happy?' Harry confirmed.

'Certainly,' I replied. 'It's not the happy people who are grateful; it's the grateful people who are happy. Does that make sense?'

'Partly...' Harry hesitated. 'I can think of things I should be grateful for, but that's not the case for everyone. I know people who have been through hell and back, whether it's losing loved ones or being disease-stricken. How can they be grateful?'

For some reason or another, the thought of my friends in Mumbai whose daughter had been diagnosed with terminal cancer came up. 'Yes, you're right, Harry. It's hard to be grateful in certain situations, and we must be careful while explaining this principle to others. When people are suffering, we should not insensitively tell them to be grateful. That would be uncompassionate. Gratitude has many layers to it. Let's understand them thoroughly.'

Incurable

What is the worst disease you can think of? For most people, it would be cancer. But they would not associate it with the young. Professor Peter Sasieni says, 'Cancer is primarily a disease of old age, with more than 60 per cent of all cases diagnosed in people aged over sixty-five.' It's a disease of the old. However, this was not the experience of my friends whose four-and-a-half-year-old daughter, Gandharvika, was diagnosed with the fastest growing tumour in humans, Burkitt's lymphoma.

Gandharvika's father, Mr Mukund Shanbag, a close friend, narrated the story to me: "'I can feel a lump in her stomach," the doctor said to me. "And it feels pretty large." The doctor paused and turned away to his computer screen, scribbling some notes. "I don't want to worry you," he continued. Those six words are enough to worry someone. I am a dentist by profession; sometimes we say this will hurt a little bit, but in reality, it may hurt a lot. "I don't want to worry you, but as your daughter is also complaining of a stomach ache I think we should take her to the hospital."

"'That's fine," I said to the doctor, who was now dialling away on his phone making arrangements for something. "Will your referral letter come by post? How long will it take?" I asked naively.

"'No, what I mean to say is, we need to get her to the hospital right now!" he said. I looked at him in panic. We had plans as a family after the appointment, but the urgency on his face signalled to me that he thought it was serious and had be attended to right away.

'After a short car ride we arrived at the hospital with the radiologist waiting there to meet us at the reception. Our doctor had made some calls. The radiologist looked familiar; he was a member of our spiritual community too. He took my daughter and me upstairs to his clinic, making small talk on the way. I was nervous, but Gandharvika was having the time of her life. This was an adventure for her. I tried to make conversation with the radiologist, but oddly enough he was also nervous. Had our doctor told him something that we did not know?

'In his clinic, the radiologist performed sonography (ultrasound) on Gandharvika. The cold gel tickled her stomach; I remember her laugh. He did not say much, but he did perform a biopsy and said that he would call us with the results. I cannot speak a sentence long enough to describe how long those forty-eight hours were. I picked up the phone when it rang, but I immediately dropped it—the doctor said that Gandharvika had a rare form of cancer. Just the word fills me with fear.

'How can one be grateful knowing that this excruciating disease is going to affect someone that they love more than their own life? My wife, Pavitra, and I found it impossible at first, but the love we received from our community exemplified how much we had to be grateful for.

'Our friends and family stepped in as soon as the treatment began. Yet the stress in the beginning was still overwhelming. Our whole family was suffering. Not only was Gandharvika going through hell, our other two children Radhika and Rasika, aged seven and two at that time, were not seeing their parents for extended periods of time. They were too young to understand what was going on. It was hard for my wife and me to be strong for them, knowing that the three of them could soon only be the two of them. I was at the hospital for almost six months continuously as Gandharvika went through the vicious cycle of chemotherapy, her blood count dropping, infection and readmission. It was a constant loop of suffering; the toughest six months of my life! What kept me sane was partly my spiritual practice, but primarily the outpouring of love from our friends around us.

'One of our friends would take my kids to their home every weekend and treat them like her own so they would not miss their mother. Both my sisters would watch my kids during the week as we rushed between work and the hospital. My father insisted that he would cook for us daily so that she would not miss home-cooked meals. Three months passed like this. This abnormal situation became our normal routine.

'By the age of four, it is said, a child starts to understand that they are an individual being, capable of having their own thoughts, aspirations and dreams. But still being children, they are not fully mature yet. That is why their response to questions like, "What do you want to be when you grow up?" is so entertaining. Walking through the dark corridors of the hospital I would wonder if I would see my daughter become a grown-up.

'In late September an issue cropped up. Gandharvika's birthday was fast approaching, and she had understandably lost all her initial patience; she wanted to go home to celebrate. The problem was that she had contracted a burning fever after her last round of chemotherapy. There was no chance she would be leaving the ward, the doctors warned us. It broke my daughter's heart. That is when we received more support.

'At lunchtime, as Gandharvika went through another round of tests, our friends and family, led by her class teacher, decorated the hospital room for her birthday as a surprise. They brought cake, party-poppers and all sorts of presents from my daughter's classmates. It was better than any birthday we could have planned! Gandharvika and our whole family were overwhelmed with joy.

'During those trying times, our spiritual teacher Radhanath Swami met with us too, enquiring about our daughter's health. He held my hands and looked into my eyes. "I am intensely praying for Gandharvika and I am intensely praying for all of you too," he said. Many people today belittle the power of prayers. But we had all the faith that the prayers and good wishes of those with deep-rooted spirituality in our community gave us the strength to deal with this turbulent phase of our life.

'Gandharvika is an energetic child; she loves to make friends. In her ward, there were many other children with the same disease whom she would play with and we would bond with the families going through the same crisis. As they say, there is strength in numbers. Nurses would comment that our daughter was different from other children; she would be praying, reading and even doing meditation. They took so much hope from this, and many even started practising spirituality themselves.

'Although we took great courage from seeing someone battle cancer together with their family, we would panic when they lost the battle. Kids who were playing with the same toys

Gandharvika had were passing away right before our eyes. Innocent children being consumed by such a devastating disease! *What if Gandharvika relapses?* was a recurrent thought for me. As I said earlier, these types of negative thoughts would pop up when I was alone, in the emptiness of the hospital listening to the cold silence. *"How would we be able to cope if we lost her?"* At times like that we could not thank those who wrapped us in love enough, helping us to heal our wounds. The gratitude that we felt for our entire spiritual community in Mumbai was a beacon that guided us and little Gandharvika through her disease. And though we thought that her disease was terminal, Gandharvika is still with us today, laughing and praying. Those who are grateful are not immune to distress. However, gratitude on many different levels offered us unlikely solace in a time of great difficulty.'

———————————

'My car is fast,' Harry said, as my consciousness returned to the conversation. 'But that was an emotional rollercoaster. It seems like Gandharvika's father had a deep connection to the quality of gratitude.'

'Indeed,' I said. 'Indeed.' I wiped my teary eyes. 'We need to make time to practise gratitude if we want to be like him.'

'Definitely,' Harry said in a sombre mood. 'I lead a very busy life . . .'

'Even more reason to truly understand gratitude. If we don't, we can miss the most beautiful aspects of our existence,' I emphasized.

Monk Mindset:

- We must have a positive state of mind when dealing with problems. Think: Is there anything positive about this situation I am in?
- Being positive does not mean we neglect the negative. We must constructively deal with negative situations while simultaneously focusing on the positive.
- Just like our tongue can be obsessed with something stuck in our teeth, our mind has a default setting to be obsessed about the negative.
- Gratitude is a state of being that allows us to see the positive. It comes from realizing that there is good in the world, that some of that good is with us and that those good things are coming from an external reality. That state of consciousness imbues us with positivity.
- Even in times of difficulty and sorrow, we can feel inner strength, when we are grateful for the support of caring friends and family.

FIVE

Press Pause

Stop and reflect on your life regularly. Pressing the pause button to practise gratitude is the way to make it a constant in your life.

When we are thankful for what we have, we become poised to receive more. Otherwise, we tend to squander opportunities that may come before us. That is as true for business as relationships. We must prioritize our gratitude. We must press pause and stop to smell the roses.

Joshua Bell

It was Hans Christian Andersen who said, 'When words fail, music speaks.' But that is only the case if you make time to listen.

Over ten years ago, a short, unassuming article was published in one of America's leading newspapers, the *Washington Post*. The paper is famous for covering the nation's political landscape, but this piece was different. It was about a social experiment that highlighted some harsh truths about the society we live in.

Most of the mid-level bureaucrats disembark at L'Enfant Plaza station, located in the heart of federal Washington. On Friday, 12 January 2007, as people slurped coffee and scarfed down doughnuts, as they scurried off to work, an inconspicuous man, in jeans and a T-shirt, stood next to a dustbin inside the station playing a violin. In a city like Mumbai, it would not be considered highly dignified for someone to play music on the street. The perception in the States is different. They are not part of the aristocracy, but not considered impoverished either. They are just seen as street performers, who can at times attract quite a crowd and media attention.

If you see someone playing music in a public area, do you stop and listen? Do you ever give any change to show your kindness? Or do you hurry past in guilt, fearful of your lack of time? That winter morning, the *Washington Post* conducted an experiment to see if people would stop for one of the finest classical musicians in the world, playing the most elegant music ever written, on one of the most expensive violins ever crafted. Would they accept their free front-row ticket to witness the musical genius or squander their opportunity, as they rushed to Capitol Hill?

The artist was the internationally renowned violinist, Joshua Bell. Thirty-nine at the time of the experiment, Bell had swapped the concert hall for the Metro hall, and an adoring audience to one who may just ignore him. Days before the experiment, Bell had filled Boston's stately Symphony Hall, where run-of-the-mill seats sell for $100. This was a test of context, perception and priorities: Would people pause to appreciate beauty when it was right in front of them?

Bell was a child prodigy. His parents, both psychologists, decided to get him formal training when they noticed that their four-year-old was making music with rubber bands—he would stretch them, opening and closing them across side-cabinets, to vary the pitch. His fame was amplified as a teenager. 'Does nothing less than tell human beings why they bother to live,' one magazine interview commented. But would the humans at the train station tell him that? Would the masses recognize this disguised genius playing perfect masterpieces on a violin worth $3.5 million?

So what do you think? A free concert by one of the world's most famous musicians! You would expect a swarm of commuters around him.

The opposite happened.

It was at three minutes that a middle-aged man glanced at Joshua for a split second, but kept walking. Thirty seconds later, a woman threw in a dollar and dashed away. It was six minutes later that someone leaned against the wall, and listened. The stats were dismal. In the forty-five minutes that Joshua Bell played, seven people stopped and hung around for at least a minute, and twenty-seven gave money to a grand total of $32. This left 1,070 people who were oblivious to the miracle happening only a few feet away from them.

The *Washington Post* recorded Bell's whole performance secretly, creating a time-lapse video of any incidents, or in this case, lack of them. 'Even at this accelerated pace, though, the fiddler's movements remain fluid and graceful; he seems so apart from his audience—unseen, unheard, otherworldly—that you find yourself thinking that he's not really there. A ghost. Only then do you see it: he is the one who is real. They are the ghosts,' the article said.

Can we label the thousand people who ignored Bell as unsophisticated? Not necessarily. The German philosopher Immanuel Kant said that the context of a situation matters. 'One's ability to appreciate beauty is related to one's ability to make moral judgements,' he said. But to do this, the 'viewing conditions must be optimal'. Art in a gallery and art in a coffee shop are going to be treated differently. In the coffee shop, the art may be more expensive and of a higher value, but there is no reason to pay attention as people sip a variety of mochaccinos. In most galleries, the 'optimal' conditions have been created to appreciate beauty. Light in the right place, enough room between the art and the viewer, a description of the piece, etc. Funnily enough, many have lost ordinary objects in art galleries later to find that people are gathered around them taking pictures thinking that they are exhibits! Context manipulates our perspective. Therefore, we cannot make judgements about people's ability to appreciate beauty because Bell *did* just look like a humdrum violinist. However, what does this say about our ability to appreciate life?

I have found that we as a people have got busier over time. We tend to exclude parts of our lives that are not directly related to hard work and accumulating wealth. The construct of the modern world is such that we have less time to press pause, and appreciate beauty. Minding their own business, stressed, with their eyes forward, people on the escalator ignoring Joshua Bell have the *capacity* to understand beauty, but it seems irrelevant to their lives so they choose not to.

If we cannot take a moment to listen to the beautiful music, played by one of the best musicians on the planet; if the drive of modern life suppresses us, so that we are deaf and blind to that spectacle, what else are we missing?

Prioritize and Practise Gratitude

The road had ground to a halt again. 'Do you see him over there?' I gestured at a man, who seemed twenty-five years old, working out on the pavement. 'A body like that does not come by chance. It must take years of practice to achieve what he has. It takes years of working late nights to create an overnight success.' It looked like his muscles had been chiselled, his arm bigger than the average man's legs. Harry tensed his left arm and visually measured his biceps. He laughed, realizing his lack of muscle in comparison to the Hercules now doing push-ups on the beach.

'Similarly, we must train the muscle of the mind. To some, gratitude is a natural disposition; to others, it's a conscious priority. But like any muscle, you must "use it or lose it". At heightened levels of practice, we do not need to consciously practise gratitude—we live in gratitude. That's a joy like no other, never missing moments like Joshua Bell!'

'How do I reach that stage?' Harry questioned eagerly.

'There is one evidence-based thing we can do. The only price is commitment and consistency. This is writing a gratitude log daily, which is based on three principles of gratitude: recognize, remember and reciprocate.'

'Wow, thank you. Please tell me more!' Harry interjected.

'Exactly, "thank" and "you" are two words that have so much power, but are overused without understanding. Let me explain,' I said. 'We should firstly recognize what good has been done to us to say "thank you". This is easy to do in the moment; like when someone holds the door for us or buys us a hot drink. The next stage is to remember what others have done for us to mean that thank you. Contemplation is by far one of the best methods to develop gratitude. Spending time with our own mind in silence, without any gadgets to stimulate us, and contemplating on who has helped us internalizes our gratitude.'

Harry hummed and nodded as if contemplating on someone at that moment.

'Finally, we should reciprocate. We should live a thank you. Saying and meaning a thank you moves to the next level through our actions. Beyond words and feelings, to truly give back is the basis of living a life of long-lasting gratitude. So what are you grateful for?'

'Well, I guess I'm grateful for this traffic jam because I have time to spend with you!'

With incessant horns surrounding us, I explained the gratitude log in more detail.

Gratitude Log

This log can be kept on your phone and written on your journey to work, or you may want to write it in your diary in a quiet space. This is a simple exercise that will take approximately ten minutes a day to do, and there are no hard or fast rules. It is best to do this activity in the morning, because starting your day with gratitude will leave you feeling positive for the rest of the day.

> ## Exercise
>
> Reflect on the last twenty-four hours and identify three to five people or situations that you are grateful for. The more descriptive you are, the easier it will be to excavate the emotion of gratitude from within you. The daily description should consist of three to five people or things you are grateful for, and once every week, it should contain three to five action points to thank the people you are grateful for.
>
> You can be grateful for anything—something as simple as someone smiling at you, giving you a seat on the train, or a co-worker buying you lunch.
>
> We cannot repay every action of kindness towards us, but we can start with the people closest to us. Pick *one* of your weekly gratitude action points and act on it. Did you thank your partner for cooking your dinner? Did you thank your mother for washing your clothes? Did you thank your partner for paying the bills? And importantly, what actions you will take to thank them. Write it down and feel the happiness you felt when the good was done unto you.

We were still bumper to bumper.

'It's a great exercise,' I said. 'It doesn't have to be long or wordy, just honest about what you are thankful for that day.'

He paused, appearing contemplative again. 'Can I ask you something personal?' he asked nervously.

It was rare for people to ask me questions about myself, but it was a refreshing change. Relationships are about give and take. 'Of course. You have shared stories of your life with me, what would you like to know about mine?'

'Have you ever been in a situation where you found it impossible to be grateful, where you could see no silver lining?'

Another silence fell between us.

'Do you want to know how my first video went viral? It was not something I wanted, and when it was happening, I certainly was not grateful,' I said, thinking about that disturbing time. I talk about the episode in the next chapter. For now, let's summarize this chapter on gratitude.

Monk Mindset:

- We must learn how to press pause and reflect on what we are grateful for. It is not good enough to say that we are too busy to be grateful.
- If we do not press pause, how many beautiful moments of our life are we missing?
- The ways to start practising gratitude are: to recognise the good that has been done unto us and say 'thank you'; to remember the good and mean it; and to reciprocate through actions of giving back and live by the same values.
- Gratitude is not merely an emotion; it is a way of life that can be learnt and practised. We must prioritize the time to practise gratitude, and one of the many ways to do it is by writing a gratitude log daily.

SIX

Why Worry

When things are beyond your control and there is nothing you can do, why worry?

One sultry evening, as I sat typing away at my laptop in my room, I received a WhatsApp message from a friend of mine. It did not look like anything out of the ordinary, but it had the potential to ruin my life. However, before I elaborate, I think it is important to tell the story of WhatsApp's success for the benefit of those readers who are not familiar with how it came about.

WhatsApp, as we all may know, is a free messaging and calling application that anyone can download, anywhere in the world except China. It was founded by Brian Acton, a software engineer who graduated from Stanford. Acton worked at Apple first and then Yahoo for around a dozen years, until in 2007, he decided to travel to South America for a year with his friend and colleague Jan Koum. On their return, both of them applied to Facebook and Twitter for jobs but both were rejected. Acton tweeted in May 2009, 'Got denied by Twitter HQ. That's okay. Would have been a long commute.' A few months later, in August 2009, he followed it up with another tweet, 'Facebook turned me down. It was a great opportunity to connect with some fantastic people. Looking forward to life's next adventure.'

And his next adventure changed the world. In the same year that he got rejected, on his birthday, WhatsApp was incorporated in Silicon Valley, California. The app grew exponentially, its success unparalleled. So much so that in 2014, Facebook decided to buy it, for a staggering $19 billion. By December 2017, WhatsApp had 1.5 billion active users!

Now that you have a clearer picture of the reach of WhatsApp, you will be able to appreciate my concern when I tell you that it was the same app that people used to share a potentially controversial video of me that went viral.

My phone buzzed. I had received a new message. A notification popped up saying I had received a video message from a friend whom I had not spoken to in years. *Interesting to get a message from him. I'll read it later*, I thought. I flipped my phone over. I did not want to be disturbed during my peak productive hours of the day. Another buzz. 'What could that be?' My mind shifted to my phone again. I managed to ignore it. In hindsight, I should have just put my phone on silent mode, because for the next hour it buzzed ceaselessly. Now I had to check what the hoo-ha was about.

I typed in my passcode and opened my WhatsApp. I saw a flood of messages drowning my home page, some from group chats I'm a part of, but many from individuals whom I had connected with over the years. The messages had one thing in common: they all contained a 3.4 MB video.

To my surprise, people had sent me a video of myself. It was a clip of a joke, edited out of context from one of the lectures I had given to an audience of 1,500 university students at our temple. Until then, a few videos of mine were gaining traction on YouTube, but tumbleweed gathered on my other social-media platforms.

I played the clip. 'In any school in India today, after ten years of working, do you know how much a teacher would save on average? Probably a lakh or two lakh rupees,' I was saying. So far, so good. No danger detected. I was sitting on a raised cushion in our main temple hall, animatedly speaking into the microphone. 'A software engineer in India today, after ten years of working, do you know how much he will earn on an average? Probably forty or fifty lakh rupees.' Nothing controversial yet. Then I went on, 'An Indian politician, not a good one, but a corrupt one, after ten years of earning through scams, will save around thirty to forty crore.' A few heads would turn at that statement; corruption in politics is a sensitive issue in India. The next group I commented on, of which I am also a part, but not in regards to wealth, is why I started receiving furious messages. 'Imagine what people who are wearing this can earn.' I grabbed my khadi saffron top. Most monks in India wear only saffron to represent their renunciation. 'One very spiritual man, a guru in India, his ten-year savings were Rs 238 crore . . . only. Another man, a spiritual, religious leader, his ten-year savings were Rs 1,177 crore only. And yet another man, again a religious leader, his savings were Rs 4,000 crore only!' The crowd was silent. Though it was just a joke and I wasn't referring to anyone in particular, a few people giggled, imagining whom

I could have been referring to. 'Choose your career wisely!' I exclaimed. The audience burst into rapturous laughter and applause. It echoed around the marble walls. A few students were rolling over, laughing hysterically.

The video was cut short there. At first, I was thrilled that people were enjoying my talk. Human nature is such that when we please others, we feel pleased ourselves. But when I scrolled through a few more messages on WhatsApp, it was clear that there was a mixed response. 'How can a saffron-clad monk like yourself say something so derogatory about India's spiritual gurus like that?' one message said. 'I found this a little offensive,' said another. Many messages expressed the same tone of disapproval.

How unfair! I thought initially. That video was part of a broader discourse to make the point that we focus on earning at the expense of our learning in our professional lives. I love to entertain the crowd, but only to teach life lessons. I am a monk after all, not a comedian.

At that point, my mind went into overdrive. 'What if this gets into the wrong hands? What if some spiritual gurus are offended? What if they complain to my ashram or the institution I am a part of or my guru? Will I bring shame to the community? Will I be banned from speaking in public? Will they sue me for defamation?' I meant no offence to those spiritual leaders. Many of them I know personally; they are pure, sincere, and use the income they generate for constructive purposes. As messages questioning my conduct rolled in, however, I could not help but think of the worst-case scenario: *What if . . . ?* I was not grateful for this situation at all!

After my initial agitation, I became defensive. I started to prepare for the inevitable, planning in my head how I would explain this to my saffron-clad brethren. I even called one of my friends who was a lawyer to draft a statement in case litigation was an issue. He assured me it would not be, but my anxiety got the better of me. Each new WhatsApp message caused my blood pressure to rise.

It did not get better in the evening. As the moon shone outside, I lay with my eyes wide open all night, clenching my thin blanket up to my chin, using it as a shield. When I was a child, I imagined a monster living under my bed, but now the only thing tormenting me was my phone charging there.

I usually rise at 4 a.m. for my morning meditations. I rubbed my eyes and rose groggily as expected. Sitting on my wooden bed, I contemplated what had happened and what could happen. Picking up my phone, I feared the worst. I adjusted to the glare and went immediately to WhatsApp. I found multiple messages sharing my own video with me, some with anger and others with love. I sighed in relief, but it had only been twelve hours since the first person sent me the tormenting clip. I was still anxious. This lasted until I received a photo message from another monk.

It is incredible how the mind works. At one moment you fear for your life, and a second later, you are entirely peaceful. Like a message from the heavens, I received a flowchart entitled: 'Why Worry'.

I pulled out the infographic from my favourites folder on my phone and showed it to Harry.

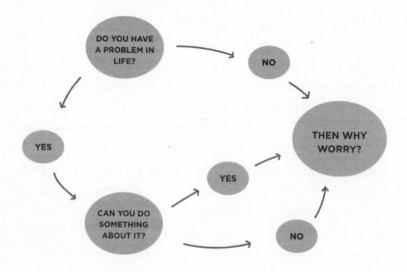

'Could you please share that with me?' he enquired.

'Definitely,' I replied, forwarding the image to him.

For years I had been practising spirituality, but I had never seen the principle of detachment from things beyond our control put so simply. Sometimes the simple explanations touch the heart the most. No fancy language or abstract concepts, just essential truths presented modestly to awaken the soul. Simple ideas are accepted universally. That is why I think a clip of my lecture on the concept of 'Why Worry' was shared on Instagram by Sean Combs (better known as P. Diddy), one of the most renowned rap artists in the world.

It's impossible to stop a clip once it's gone viral on the internet. When we have a problem beyond our control, we have to turn to our spiritual strength and ask, 'Why Worry?' Whether or not we can do something about it, our response should not be anxiety. Learning to detach ourselves from situations that are outside our control is an imperative skill to learn for personal growth. This is not to say I favour laziness—we should do everything in our power to try to rectify the situation, but after that, we have to take our attention away from the unpleasant circumstance.

What we see as bad at one point in time can turn out to be good for us, and what we see as good at another point in time can turn out to be bad for us. Most things in life are beyond our control; we should not judge any situation by its face value. A video that I thought would disrupt my life as I knew it turned out to be the greatest blessing. It allowed me to kick-start my journey to be able to try to help inspire millions across the globe through my social-media presence and even brought me the opportunity to convey my message through this book.

So, I repeat, whatever situations may come our way, analyse: Is this in my control? Regardless of the answer that follows, the reply should always be, 'Why Worry!'

I noticed that Harry looked relieved when I talked about this. I meditated on how when we hear things that are meaningful, our doubts are dispelled. The easiest way to bring clarity to our life is to seek guidance from people who possess clarity.

'Spiritual strength . . .' he brought up. His questions were not finished. 'To get to that level of detachment or state of gratitude, you need what you called spiritual strength. How do you get that?' I was surprised at how attentively he had been listening even as he drove. When we are desperate, our senses become heightened and we become more attentive.

'Sometimes when we get engrossed in a problem, we feel trapped in our own minds,' I said. 'In that state, we constantly regurgitate our issues, causing us a lot of emotional pain.

A spiritual process gives us the ability to come out of this mental loop and helps transform the greatest difficulties into opportunities.'

Monk Mindset:

- Some things in life are beyond our control. When we are in that situation, we feel overwhelmed as we try everything in our power to control it. But that is useless!

- The founders of WhatsApp did not get jobs at Twitter and Facebook when they applied, which worked out in their favour in the future. Hence, what we see as bad at one point in time can turn out to be the best thing to happen to us.

- Just as I could not control the virality of my 'out-of-context' video, similarly there are many situations in life that are out of our control.

- Think: Is this in my control? If yes, you can do something about it. If no, then you cannot do anything about it. Therefore, in both circumstances, why worry?

SEVEN

Spiritual Practice

Spiritual practice is the foundation of our happiness. It guides us in times of turmoil and grounds us in times of joy.

Spirituality is based on the premise that we live in this world, but we are not from it. Many of our problems lie in not understanding our fundamental identity: we are not human beings having spiritual experiences; we are spiritual beings having human experiences. It's impossible to realize this principle theoretically. We can attend hundreds of lectures and read volumes of books; but this is inadequate without us committing to a spiritual practice, or sadhana as it is known in Sanskrit.

The simplest way to explain spiritual practice is to describe the hierarchy of connections. At any moment, we can be making three kinds of connections:

Outside ourselves: The majority of our time is spent in connecting with the world—networking, relationships, our work. It's all crucial, but can lead us astray if we have no inner direction. The fear of missing out, thinking that the grass is greener elsewhere, and living a life out of balance are all symptoms of having incorrectly prioritized happiness outside of ourselves.

Inside ourselves: Beyond our everyday lives, many look for solace within. People struggling with life, those trying to work on themselves to conquer the external world, those curious about their inner world, and occasionally, a few of those seeking the truth—these are the types of people who will take the journey within.

Above ourselves: Those simply voyaging within can get frustrated by their lack of progress or direction. They can feel as though they're on a ship travelling at 70 knots, but without a compass. Connecting above ourselves means re-establishing our relationship with God, or something higher than ourselves. God is One, and is identified differently across different cultures. Therefore, it is not about connecting to my God or your God, it is about connecting to our God. When this happens, it is as if a light bulb is getting connected to an entire powerhouse. A bulb on its own is just a piece of glass with a tungsten filament; it needs an electrical charge to experience light and give light to others. Similarly, it is our relationship with something higher than ourselves that can give us love and allow us to give love to others.

Harry listened as I explained further, 'Just as there are many paths to get to our destination, there are many ways of connecting to God that transcend religious and sectarian boundaries. Many people practise prayer, a simple yet deeply effective method to become self-realized. I do practise prayer, but my preferred method for developing spiritual strength is through meditation.

'Out of the many types of meditation, I practise mantra meditation. This means I spend some time daily focusing my mind on sacred sounds, chanting the name of God, by which we can free ourselves of anxiety. Modern science recognizes the huge benefits of meditation: relieving us of stress, giving us a sense of purpose, thus enabling us to become more creative, among many other benefits. However, ancient eastern literature gives us deeper insight.

'Meditation is like a plane: It first takes you high, then far away and then further away imperceptibly. I see meditation like a plane because when you take off, you immediately start gaining altitude. We experience worry and anxiety in life because we take things out of perspective. Meditation enables us to look down at all our anxieties, problems and worries through a higher vantage-point, thus giving us a great sense of peace and calmness.

'The deeper effect is that meditation carries us far. It completely transforms our character, develops the best of qualities within us and allows us to experience self-realization. Through meditation we become the best versions of ourselves. But this takes time and is often imperceptible. For example, if you look outside the window on a plane it does not look like you are moving very fast. But eight hours later, you're landing halfway across the world.

'Meditation becomes difficult because of our mind. It is said that the mind is like a restless monkey, always jumping from one thought to another. It does not become peaceful just because you say so. It needs to be controlled. Therefore, meditation is a discipline that helps us control the mind. For example, the trains of Mumbai keep the city's economy moving. But what keeps them travelling is the fact that they are bound by the tracks, schedule and destinations. Similarly, the mind without being bound by the discipline of meditation will not be able to reach its destination. Some days it will feel like meditating, and some days it will not—'

'Even understanding the concept of meditation takes time. I know many executives and celebrities practise it, but I've never felt like I have the time,' Harry interrupted. He seemed to be feeling overwhelmed at the variety of concepts I had presented.

'People with no time to spare need it the most.' I chuckled. 'I am now able to practise meditation for two hours a day. It was not like that in the beginning. I could cope with only ten minutes a day when I initially started and that didn't seem so daunting.'

Harry nodded, then asked, 'After all this time, have you noticed any changes in your character?'

'I have, quite honestly. One doesn't have to wait to see the effects of meditation in the afterlife—we can see them in this life if we practise it diligently enough and under the right guidance.'

He seemed impressed with that answer.

'Do you remember what I said about the importance of gratitude earlier?' I asked.

'Sure.'

'People who meditate develop a habit of practising sincere gratitude, which helps them in all their relationships. It is a "relationship-strengthening emotion" because it requires us to see how we've been supported and affirmed by other people.'

Harry began to fidget with the steering wheel again. 'What's on your mind?' I asked.

'I was thinking about how my wife and I treat each other,' he said, ready to take our conversation forward, and I knew it was time to tell him about the second wheel of life.

Monk Mindset:

- We are not human beings having spiritual experiences; we are spiritual beings having human experiences. We are not this body; we are a spiritual being.
- We need to understand the hierarchy of connections. Ultimately, we must connect to something above ourselves. This can give us the power to spread happiness and joy around the world.
- There are many ways to connect to this higher power. We may have our own, which is great, and we should go deeper into it. One of the most effective methods that has worked really well for me is mantra meditation.

WHEEL 2
RELATIONSHIPS

EIGHT

Speaking Sensitively

We should deal with each other sensitively; our attitude towards life affects how we act in our relationships.

'What do you mean how you treat your wife?' I asked him, alarmed. I had been to their house and found nothing amiss. Was there something he wasn't sharing?

'It's not what it sounds like,' he said, blushing. 'It is just that we are constantly fighting and bickering. She always wants to change things about me, and I end up leaving the room when she starts with her suggestions.'

I was quite taken aback by his comments. How people behave in public can be very different from how they are in their private lives.

'Just a few minutes ago I was experiencing the warmth in the exchanges between you two,' I said.

'I suppose we act differently depending on whose company we are in.' He paused for a moment. 'How can we maintain the "spark" that we once had? What you witnessed at my home today was what it was constantly like in America when we were together, but it slowly started to fizzle out. Why does this happen?'

There was a series of things I wanted to say. I started by comforting him, 'This happens with all relationships, not just in marriages. If we are not proactive in our relationships, they start to seem dry and become cumbersome. We have to have respect for the other person, which is reflected in how sensitively we treat them.'

I had another anecdote to share:

Attitude Does Not Discriminate

I am not always flying around the world giving seminars. In Mumbai, I like to be just another monk; one of the many.

Before I decided to dedicate my life to being a monk, I was a pampered boy growing up in a middle-class family in Pune. Like most children around the world, I feel I had (and have) the best mother. She took care of everything—she would cook only what I wanted to eat and would wash all my clothes. I was never kept waiting for anything. Therefore, you can imagine how shocking and worrisome it was for her when I decided to pursue the life of a monk. Who would cook for me? Who would clean for me? Who would wash my clothes?

The answers to those questions were: cooking was done communally, but for everything else, you were on your own. It was a steep learning curve. Washing my clothes for the first time was an ordeal. We did not have a washing machine; it was just two buckets and a handful of soap. This was the old-school method of washing your clothes: let your garments soak for thirty minutes in detergent and water and then rinse them in another bucket of clean water. No need for a gym membership; this style of washing made for sufficient exercise. In fact, I was pleasantly surprised at my biceps getting bigger simply from squeezing the excess water from my clothes!

One day, I went to wash my clothes that had already been soaking in the soapy water. I was in a rush; I had to deliver a talk in Borivali, on the other side of the city. I now had to face the tribulation of rinsing my clothes. I opened the tap and water gurgled through the steel pipes and straight on to the floor of the bathroom. Reacting swiftly, I kicked a bucket under the tap.

'What were you doing?' a grave voice asked from behind me. It was one of the older monks.

'Just washing my clothes,' I replied respectfully.

'Yes, I can see that. But what were you doing?' he asked again.

'Just . . . washing my clothes,' I repeated. His eyes rolled and he frowned.

'Yes, I can see that. But what were you doing?' he said enunciating each word slowly.

'Just washing my clothes!' I retorted, losing my patience. 'What's the problem?' I was going to be late for an important talk I was meant to deliver.

'Why did you kick the bucket?' he asked.

'It's just a bucket; I had to get it under the tap quickly. It's no big deal.'

'No big deal?' he questioned. 'It *is* a big deal. Gaur Gopal, I want to share with you what I have learnt about relationships. When we treat inanimate objects, like buckets or our possessions, with disrespect or insensitivity, we will end up treating people the same. At one point in my life, I seemed to be losing a lot of my friends and I heard this advice from one of my guides. Insensitivity becomes part of our general attitude, and our instinct does not discriminate between things and people. Hence, when we treat our things badly, we might notice that insensitivity gradually creeping into our relationships with the people around us.'

Then he patted me on my back, smiling, and walked away singing an Indian bhajan. I folded my hands in reverence and turned off the tap to reflect on what had happened. This whole universe is connected, as are the parts of our life. When we treat things with disrespect, we may start doing the same with the people we love. All aspects of our life are integrated.

In modern culture, it is common to use things once and throw them away. For example, plastic cups. In 2016, the Ellen MacArthur Foundation reported at the World Economic Forum that we will have more plastic in the sea than fish by 2050 if we continue producing the substance at this rate. If we can have this mentality with our things, we may end up introducing disposability in our relationships as well.

The memory of my mother, who is a voracious reader, reading the classic books of Indian literature to me is still vivid in my mind. She would be telling me (on the verge of acting out) exhilarating stories of gods and demons fighting over Mother Earth and of Mother Ganges flowing towards the sea, sustaining all forms of life through this journey. She would also tell me about Mother Cow, who is considered sacred in our tradition. The Earth and the River Ganges are inanimate and the cow is but an animal. But in the mystical culture of the East, we are taught to treat them just like we would our own mother. With that level of respect for things, it's easy to see why people who practise genuine spirituality are typically known to have strong interpersonal bonds.

'I've never heard it explained like that before. But you know something? Ronaldo and Messi would get the shock of their lives if they heard this story. Their whole life is based on kicking a football and scoring goals.' Harry chuckled.

'It's not about kicking or not kicking,' I said. 'Everything has its utility and must be used in that particular way. Would you ever use a ruler to measure the temperature? I hope not. We should use things for the purpose they have been designed for but should treat them with the utmost dignity, value and respect.'

'Hmmm. But I tend to compartmentalize my life,' Harry said. 'I don't see every aspect of my life as fully connected. I am used to putting things in boxes like, this is my work, these are my relationships and this is my spirituality,' he said, using his hands to illustrate his point.

'There are two sides to that. For practical purposes, we will often benefit from putting things into compartments but we should know that the way we act in one area of our life can have dire consequences in another.'

'I suppose so. In conflicts with my wife, maybe I have a role to play. Maybe I am being insensitive to her. It takes two hands to clap—maybe she is just mirroring my reaction in the way she responds to me,' he said.

'Yes, at times, we incite the response that people give us. When we look at them while keeping in mind that we also need to improve things about ourselves, it is easier to assess how we should behave with others,' I replied. 'Let's talk about how we can see the positive in our relationships.'

Monk Mindset:

- We must be sensitive with our words and actions. Being sensitive means to think about how the other person may feel before we say or do something.
- How do we practise being sensitive? We must treat even inanimate objects with consideration and respect. If we do not, then the mentality of insensitivity may become a part of our general attitude.
- One's instinct or general attitude does not discriminate between things and people. Treating things badly can affect our attitude negatively, which may percolate into our relationships.

NINE

A Virtuous Vision

There are many ways to perceive others. We should start choosing the one that magnifies the positive and avoids the negative.

With car horns blaring around us and crows squawking above us, we were still stuck, but were also edging closer to our destination. We still did not know what was causing the traffic jam.

I was about to begin speaking when a bumblebee flew into the car. Bees are usually harmless, but in such a confined space, Harry and I both threw our heads back against the head rests and remained completely still. Our yellow-and-black friend buzzed around the dashboard of the car. Mesmerized by the jasmine-scented car fragrance flowing out of the vents, it was probably looking for flowers. When it realized there was no pollen in our vehicle, it flew away merrily, singing the song all bees sing.

'That was close,' Harry said, now visibly relieved. 'That bee was huge!'

'I'm just thankful it was not its passionate and angry cousin,' I said, referring to wasps. 'The bee teaches us so much,' I went on, as a thought came to my mind. 'They are always looking for the nectar that flowers possess and avoid lingering where there is dirt. We should be like the bee—always seeing the best in people and choosing to avoid their faults.'

'How is it possible to do that? It seems too tough to me, given how my relationships are,' Harry replied.

'It all depends on what we look for. I have learnt that there are five different ways we can perceive people in our relationships. Let me tell you a bit more about it.'

Type 1: A Person Who Cannot See the Good at All

The first type of person only sees the bad and tends to magnify it out of proportion. Possibly arising out of spite, dislike or insecurity, they just cannot see any good qualities that another person may possess. As much as you may try to explain to them about someone's goodness, they refuse to change their opinion. They see a speck of dirt on someone's face and look at it as if the entire body of the person were bathed in mud.

I am reminded of a story that I heard some time back. There was a young couple who lived in a nice home in a beautiful neighbourhood. For some reason, the wife just did not like the woman who was their next-door neighbour. One morning, as they were having breakfast, the lady looked out of the window and saw her neighbour hanging clothes on the clothes line.

'Look at that,' she said to her husband. 'Did you see how dirty their clothes are even after washing them? I am shocked that a middle-aged housewife like her doesn't know how to wash clothes clean. Maybe she should go back to her mom's home and take lessons on how to wash correctly.'

Her husband listened silently. Every single time her neighbour would hang her clothes to dry, the young woman wouldn't miss a chance to make some sly comments.

After a few weeks, the wife saw her neighbour hanging clothes on the clothes line again. But this time something was different.

'Did you see that? Amazing!' the surprised wife said to her husband. 'Finally her clothes are clean! I am sure she did not wash them. Someone else must have done it for her!' Without even getting up from his seat to look at the neighbour's clothes, the husband responded, 'You know something, darling? I got up early this morning and washed our windows.'

Isn't it a fact that what we see in others depends on the window we are looking through? Washing our own windows can change our vision.

But Type-1 people don't even agree that their windows are dirty, what to speak of cleaning them. They not only continue to perceive the clean laundry as dirty but also keep bad-mouthing it.

Type 2: A Person Who Sees Both, the Good and the Bad, But Chooses to Neglect the Good

The second type of person sees the good and bad in people, but makes a conscious decision to neglect the good and focus on the bad. Like some people have selective hearing, people of this type have a selective mindset.

Many of my videos have gone viral over the last few years, but they do not come close to matching the popularity of dog videos. We tend to be infatuated by dogs, so much so that we are left wondering what we did to deserve this faithful friend. An interesting story reveals how devoted dogs are. I don't know how far it is true, though:

A man was once buying groceries from a supermarket. He was pushing his trolley while looking at his scribbled list when he crashed into another trolley. 'Sorry!' he exclaimed automatically. But what he saw shocked him. It was a dog pushing the other shopping trolley and picking up a variety of things! Amazed, he followed the dog around from aisle to aisle, snooping on his every move. The dog picked up fruits, chocolate, bread, pasta: a bag's worth of provisions. Then he went up to the cashier and pulled out a few dollar bills to make the payment. The monotonous cashier was unfazed. It seemed as if he was familiar with this furry friend. The man then saw that the cashier gave the dog $10 less. The dog barked and tugged at the cashier's trouser leg until he gave him the correct balance. *How is this possible?* the man thought, standing there, gobsmacked. *I have to find out who owns this intelligent dog!*

The man followed the dog all the way to its home on the fifteenth floor of an apartment block. You guessed it—the dog pressed the correct floor on the elevator, reached a dark-blue door and dropped the shopping. He then began to scratch on the door, making a whining sound to get the attention of his owner. After some time, the owner opened the door and started shouting at the dog. 'You useless, ungrateful good-for-nothing animal! I hope you got everything!' Then they both went inside. The man was even more bewildered now. Did the dog's owner really just say that? Curious, he knocked on the door three times, twiddling his thumbs, anxious to ask the owner why he had shouted at his genius dog. It opened.

'Yes?' the owner asked rudely.

'Err, sir, I just had a question. I noticed that your dog did all the shopping from the supermarket for you, managed to get the correct change from the cashier, walked all the way back to this building, pressed the right number on the elevator—he is unbelievable! Why did you shout at him? I have to know why.'

'Yes. All that's normal for him. But this is the second time he's forgotten the keys to the house. It's pathetic, I had to get up and open the door!' The man stood outside the apartment with his mouth wide open in disbelief at what he had just heard.

Isn't this the story of our lives? Our friends and family are doing so many good things, but we neglect them and focus solely on the negatives. Wonderful things are occurring all around us, and within the people we love, but this type of person can only think about how the other forgot the key!

Type 3: A Person Who Sees the Good and the Bad and Is Neutral to Both

The next type is a person who sees good and bad in others; s/he doesn't focus on the bad, but is unconcerned about the good as well. Such people are disconnected from everyone and everything, either due to their self-absorption or indifference, and they just don't care. It is nearly impossible to find such a person.

Type 4: A Person Who Sees Good and Bad, but Consciously Chooses to Neglect the Bad

Then there are those who see the good and bad but consciously choose to neglect the bad and focus on the good. It is tough for people to live by this as they have to make the conscious effort to stay away from the natural human tendency to see the bad. It can take a lot of work to continuously see the good.

A recent article about the late industrialist Aditya Birla featured in the 'Speaking Tree' section of the *Times of India* succinctly highlights the characteristics of this type of person.

Aditya Birla was the CEO of the multibillion-dollar company Hindalco Industries. The article is about one of his senior executives who lost the company millions of dollars by mistake. Any other leader would have fired—if not sued—the employee, but not Aditya Birla. Before he had a meeting with him, Birla took out a notepad and wrote a title at the top: *Points in favour of this employee.* He then made a list of all the strengths this man had, including the time he had made the company millions of dollars. Aditya Birla had consciously chosen to shift his attention to all the good that this executive had done for the company before making any judgement or dealing with the mistake.

As news spread throughout the company that Birla did not sack this employee, a philosophy and culture of sensitive dealings evolved within the organization. Another senior executive in the company wrote, 'Whenever I am tempted to reprimand someone, I convince myself to sit down and write a list of all the good qualities they have. This may not necessarily change my decision, but it helps me put things into perspective and control my anger.'

To focus on the good and deal with the bad is a principle that can save relationships and help us make the right decision.

Type 5: A Person Who Cannot See the Bad at All; They See the Slightest Good and Magnify It

This stage can only be possible for God, or for one who has reached the heights of spirituality. To see only the good in someone's character, or to magnify the slight good to the point where it overshadows their ills, is a great feat but one which is impractical for most of us to follow.

The ideal state for our relationships to flourish is to come to stage four. The human condition is such that we love to gossip about the faults of others; we open our eyes and see only dirt. However, with practice, we can come to the stage of seeing both the good and the bad, and consciously make the decision to focus on the good and neglect the bad.

'I have never heard an explanation like that before!' Harry exclaimed.

'It's not my analysis, I heard it from Srila Prabhupada's followers,' I replied.

'Can you clarify one thing? How do you totally neglect the bad?'

'Neglecting the bad does not mean that we do not deal with it practically. It just means that we do not allow our mind to focus on and hover over the bad.'

'Exactly!' Harry seemed to agree with the point vehemently, though I don't think he fully understood it.

'With my wife, I tend not to neglect the bad, but deal with it . . .' He paused. 'I try to deal with it sensitively in my opinion, but it always creates an awkward air around us and leaves her feeling hurt, I think. Then she starts making sarcastic comments to me. Then I tell her not to, but the vicious cycle starts again. It's frustrating!'

Monk Mindset:

- Seeing the best in people can be challenging at times, especially when we are in constant proximity to them.
- We can perceive people in the following five ways:
    o See only bad and magnify it.
    o See good and bad, neglect the good and focus on the bad.
    o See good and bad, and be neutral to both.
    o See good and bad, choose to focus on the good and neglect the bad.
    o See the good and magnify it.
- The ideal state is the fourth stage, in which one's relationships flourish.
- Reaching the fourth stage takes consistent hard work and practice.

TEN

Correcting Cautiously

Corrective feedback can make or break our relationships.

'Most of the time our frustration comes from improper dealings in our relationships,' I said, trying to console Harry. 'And this stems from our poor communication, whether it's our body language, actions or words. We must take full responsibility for our relationships,' I continued.

'But if I'm always thinking about what to say to not upset my wife, that would make life miserable and so calculated,' Harry retorted.

I sighed. 'Harry, yes, we must choose our words carefully when we are correcting others, but before that we must learn to invest appreciation in them.'

I settled down to explain in detail.

Investment before Withdrawal

I was once invited to speak on the topic of "Indian Culture Empowering Work–Life Balance". The venue was what you would expect it to be. A large, round auditorium, a grand stage lined with a velvet red carpet and 150 executives from stock exchanges around the world. It was a prestigious event, and I felt honoured to be invited to speak there. A point that I made there seemed to resonate with the high-flying audience. I said, "Our mutual funds and our relationships have one thing in common: we must invest in both before we can withdraw." And this is how it is—many times we forget to invest appreciation and love into a person before we correct them. This can leave them feeling demotivated and not cherished. Learning the art of appreciation is vital for building healthy relationships. I realized this when I was travelling in Nepal.

'I remember how, even as my teeth chattered and my body shivered, my eyes gazed at the beauty that surrounded me. It was bitterly cold in Muktinath, at the foot of the Thorong La mountain pass in the Himalayas. Muktinath is a sacred place for Hindus and Buddhists alike. For the Hindus, it is the place where the natural form of Lord Vishnu is found downstream at Kali Gandaki. And for the Buddhists it is a place where important gods and goddesses have resided.

'A few monks, including myself, had taken a group of families to this beautiful part of the world for a spiritual retreat. After spending some time discussing the significance of the place we were at, we returned to our accommodation. The purpose of this trip was not only to visit all the places of spiritual virtue but, more importantly, to spend time with these families. There is no substitute for spending quality time with each other, and I have found that open communication with people in the midst of nature can do wonders to strengthen bonds. There could have been no better backdrop for this than the Himalayas!

'As I returned to the townhouse that we had rented, I flicked open my laptop to check my email. Although time had stopped for me while I was away on this spiritual retreat, it had not for people in Mumbai who had pressing issues to discuss with me. As I scrolled through my inbox, scanning for anything imperative, a flagged email caught my eye. "Your visa to Ukraine has been approved. Your passport is ready to be collected from Delhi, or will take five working days to reach your chosen address."

'*Five working days?* I panicked. Another monk and I were meant to fly to Ukraine in three days' time, as soon as we landed in Mumbai. There was no way I could miss my flight to Ukraine; my spiritual teacher Radhanath Swami had personally asked me to visit.

'I immediately got up. I started planning in my head. I ran into the communal area of the house. Everyone was laughing and warming up over some herbal tea, their woollen hats and gloves drying on the radiators. Thinking it was appropriate, I asked one of the senior monks, out of courtesy, if I could fly to Delhi slightly earlier to pick up my passport from the Ukrainian consulate. The bus and train journey to Delhi from Kathmandu was a gruelling thirty-four hours. A flight was only a couple of hours, saving me valuable time in my race to get to Eastern Europe.

'"How are you planning to go?" he asked me while sipping on hot ginger tea.

'"Flight, it's only a few hours," I said confidently.

'"And who's going to pay for that flight?"

'I sensed that this was not going to go my way. "Well . . ." not wanting to say *the temple*, which was already low on funds, "I have to go because my passport is in Delhi. We won't reach Ukraine in time if I do not get my passport by tomorrow morning," I pleaded.

'The noise of people talking quietened as they homed in on our conversation. The senior monk put his tea down.

'"I do not think it's a good idea. You can travel with us by train to Delhi and then proceed to Ukraine a few days later," he said authoritatively.

'Our tickets were already booked. However, I left it at that and went to my room to let things settle down. In the evening, the senior monk gave a small lecture to the group, narrating stories about the sites we had seen. As we approached dinner time, I brought up the topic with him again. It was vital that I get to Ukraine.

'He got up and started to raise his voice in front of everybody. "I already told you that this is not possible. Why are you bringing it up again? Don't you have any manners?" He went on ridiculing me for what seemed like five long minutes. It was humiliating. All these families knew me personally; their kids looked up to me as a role model, and here I was being slandered publicly.

'I walked away to my room. I paced up and down our 3-metre-long room with bunk beds on either side, panting shallowly. My eyes teared up. Thoughts rushed through my head, *How could somebody speak to me like that? I thought we were friends! He doesn't understand how important my flight to Ukraine is!* In anger, it is so easy to lash out. When our ego is crushed, our emotions run wild. I controlled myself, took a deep breath in and said a prayer, silently—I decided to press pause.

'He had a point. The temple was tight on finances, it was inappropriate to ask the families travelling with us for funding, and I could not just abandon them on this trip. These were the practical reasons I listed to help me calm down. It helped, but only slightly. I closed my eyes, and like a flashback, I remembered all my years in the ashram that the senior monk had nurtured me and was a friend to me when times were tough. He was the one who made me feel like the ashram was my home. He had not treated me this way before during all this time that I had known him. He had always been investing love, kindness and trust in me. It was not like him to lash out like this. Was there something on his mind?

'I washed my face and returned to where everybody had congregated. It smelled like tomato soup and freshly baked bread, but as I walked into the room, the tension was palpable. I went in as if nothing had happened and behaved like I always did. He glanced at me and our eyes met—our subtle method of apologizing and forgiving. You could see people sighing with relief. I had forgiven him; we did not bring up the issue again.

'The Kathmandu bus station was bustling in the morning: people selling tea from metal containers, porters running with people's bags on their carts, and tourists in shorts and huge cameras being harassed by kids who wanted a few rupees. It was a scene similar to most South Asian transport terminals. We travelled by bus for ten hours to Gorakhpur, where our journey would continue by train.

'It was a quick transition between bus and train. We had tickets for a sleeper-class cabin, where seats could turn into three-tiered bunk beds. I was excited to see the blue berths as my neck was slightly sore from sitting in the bus for half a day. I settled down next to the window and watched as the train picked up speed and weaved through the divine countryside.

'Thirty minutes into the journey, the senior monk came and solemnly sat down next to me. He held my hand, and with tears flowing down his face, apologized for how he had treated me. I couldn't help but cry with him—I had never seen him so emotional. When we see people we love feeling upset, we naturally feel upset, too. I also apologized to him, saying that I should not have pushed him and that his concerns were valid. He did not accept my apology and insisted that it was all his fault. Indeed, true forgiveness contributes to forming the strongest bonds between friends.

'A few weeks later, when we got together with all the families for an event, we asked them what the highlights of their trip to Nepal had been. We were expecting them to say that they loved the mystic temples, the scenery of Kathmandu or even our lectures—none of them said that. They all unanimously agreed that the highlight had been seeing the friendship between me and the senior monk. From an unpleasant exchange to deep forgiveness, they were astonished at the depth of our bond. To this day, he remains one of my closest friends.

'Only when we invest in people can we correct them. Sometimes this is done strongly, but we are all human. Mistakes happen and tempers are lost. But if our investments in others are strong, if we give them the care, love and appreciation they deserve, these little withdrawals come across as sprinkles of rain and not as torrential monsoons. This does not mean that we never give corrective feedback, but we need to learn the art of doing it correctly. Let me explain:

Corrective Feedback: An Art

'Beyond any other need, the greatest longing of every individual is *to give love and to be loved*. It is our relationships that allow this mantra to come to fruition. However, it is surprising that the relationships we cherish and keep so close to our heart can easily be neglected and abused. For the most part, this is not done on purpose, but out of ignorance and an inability to understand how one should behave. We may have the right intentions but giving advice inappropriately may do more harm than good. That is why we must learn to do it properly, and it takes practice and introspection to develop this ability. Any time you feel the need to give corrective feedback to someone, think of these four questions:

Am I the right person to give corrective feedback?

'Is it appropriate for you to correct that person? We would all scream at someone else's child who is about to injure itself, but we are not talking of those exceptional situations. In any other situation would you give corrective feedback to someone else's child? Would you give feedback to another's spouse? In most situations, you would not. Therefore, we have to think, am I the right person to give this feedback or is someone else better suited? Am I a relative? Am I a friend? Am I an authority in any way to give correct feedback? If the answer to any of these questions is yes, then you can proceed to the next one.

Do I have the right motive to give corrective feedback?

'It is said that we can control two things in our life, our desires and our motives. Our desires govern *what* we want and our motives tell us *why* we want it. In many cases, we may correct others because we want to settle old accounts. We may have a grudge against them and we may use the opportunity to correct them, simply to exact our vengeance. But this should not be our motive. It should be to help them as a friend. We should be conscientious that our motive is appropriate; we want to help them come out of the wrong they are doing. Feedback from a place of love may seem unpalatable, but it tastes the sweetest if done appropriately and has the right effect.

Do I know the right way to give corrective feedback?

'Jack was an electrical engineer. His days were exhausting and mentally demanding; he would need to deal with complex physics as part of his design work. One oversight could lead to his company losing crores of rupees, or worse, him getting fired. It was a Thursday and Jack was the most tired he had ever been. All he wanted to do was to eat dinner with his wife, Jill. As you may have guessed by now, this story is made up but I promise you, it serves a purpose! Jill was a chef by profession and loved treating her husband to her new, experimental dishes. She was excited for him to come home so he could taste her new recipe for soup.

'When Jack came home, his face was drained of colour from fatigue. He threw his briefcase on the floor, loosened his tie, greeted his wife and sat at the dining table. 'This soup looks delicious,' he said.

'"It's a special recipe that I have been working on all day. I wanted you to taste it first," a giddy Jill said.

'Jack took a ladle and poured himself the creamy red soup. He looked up at his beaming wife, watching his every move. She slid a spoon across the table for him and then put both hands under her chin, elbows on the dining table, and leaned forward. Jack slurped a spoonful. Tomatoes, good. Chillies, good. Salt, bad. The soup was totally bland.

'What would you do in this situation? You've just had a terrible day at work. How would you tell your wife about the poor quality of her cooking?

'Thankfully, Jack "engineered" a plan on the spot. He grabbed another spoon from the cutlery drawer and said, smiling, "It's been so long since I've lovingly fed you. Come and try this." Saying so, he fed her some soup.

'"Oh! I forgot the salt." She jumped up, arriving at the conclusion by herself.

'Jack could have easily criticized his wife's soup using unkind words. Instead, he chose to give his feedback with sensitivity. People are usually resilient. They can stand being wrong, but only when it is pointed out to them with love. Being blunt and abusive can be emotionally draining for both, and the person receiving the feedback switches off after some time. As is commonly said, "It was not what you said, it's how you said it." Our tone of voice, body language and facial expressions account for more than the words we use.

Is it the right time?

'The most ironic moment of my life occurred at Soho Square, central London. I had just finished giving a one-hour presentation on overcoming fault-finding, and a man came up to me at the end and said, "Thank you for the class, but I really hated it." I sat there stunned as he listed *in detail* what he did not like about the class and my delivery. I felt as Jill would have if Jack had shrieked about the bland soup. It was horrible to experience someone giving me harsh feedback immediately after I had poured my heart and soul out. It may have been the case that my talk was atrocious, but like a man who misses his flight, this person had got the timing all wrong. If he had said the same things to me a few days later, we would have both been in a better state of mind. We should not simply let our anger loose—we should explain it. When we express what we feel, we do so at the risk of seeming unpleasant, but when we take the time to explain our emotions to people, they might be able to empathize with us. The bottom line: hot heads do not give good feedback—choose a better time.

'Taking the time to ask these four questions before giving somebody correctional feedback can change one's life. To understand them deeply, contemplation and discussion with someone more experienced than oneself are required as every situation is different. The principles remain the same in every situation, but the application may vary on a case-to-case basis, depending on the gravity of the situation or even our relationship with the person. We would not correct our spouses in the same manner we would our children. One size does not fit all, neither do our methods to correct.'

'This practice will take some time to implement, and form into a habit,' Harry said, as he looked away from the steering wheel momentarily to look at me.

'You're right.' I nodded. 'Having the knowledge of something is far from mastering it. Giving feedback badly is an addiction. Just as a smoker *knows* that cigarettes can kill him but smokes nonetheless, similarly the way we interact with others becomes an addiction. We know when we are careless, but our habits *force* us to act in a certain way.

Harry's expression reverted to one I had seen earlier in this car journey. His face dropped and his breathing slowed. 'When I return from the office I am usually stressed,' he whispered. 'I am not like that guy in the story. I really lash out over trivial issues. I did not realize that all these small acts of contempt could lead up to what happened the other night. Lalita and I got into a huge argument over something trivial that I can't even remember now. The fight reached its crescendo, and she screamed at me saying she wanted a divorce! Divorce? How can she want a divorce after all we have been through?' At this point, Harry was talking to himself, churning his emotions. 'What would my family think if I got divorced? Would my friends judge me? I suppose being careless about little things can really prove to be fatal. But I really do love my wife, and I know I need to change, but how can I ever forgive her for saying something so cruel and hurtful?'

Another question loaded with emotion, I thought to myself. I looked out of the car window. We were driving past couples holding hands and walking along the coastline. I said, 'Let me tell you about something worse.'

Monk Mindset:

- Saying things in anger damages our relationships. Hence, we should try to avoid doing so.
- If we need to give corrective feedback, we should invest tonnes of praise and trust into a person before doing so.
- Think: With regard to the story in Nepal, I could deal with the emotional hurt because I realized how much the individual correcting me had done for me in the past.
- Corrective feedback is an art. It has four principles. Ask yourself:
  o Am I the right person to give corrective feedback?
  o Do I have the right motive to give corrective feedback?
  o Do I know the right way to give corrective feedback?
  o Is it the right time?
- The smooth implementation of these four principles takes time because giving corrective feedback insensitively has become an addictive habit for many.

ELEVEN

Forgiveness

Forgiveness is a complex concept. We must understand it thoroughly to be able to internalize it.

You cannot drive in any city without seeing billboards everywhere. Every few minutes, you see a new purchase that you *have* to make to survive, socially. They leave nothing to the imagination any more.

'How we market our products is just a reflection of how our view of the human condition in general has changed over the years,' I told Harry. 'We no longer bother with the subtle intricacies and niceties in our relationships—we think about people in terms of their purpose or utility, and hence, our interactions are driven by that intention. We think about products the same way.' The look on Harry's face was now a mixture of intrigue and "what are you on about?"

'We live in a world of quick fixes. We can microwave our food, and it instantly becomes warm. We can stream our movies, and watch them whenever we like. We can book our tickets to anywhere using our phones. Instant travel arrangements! No problem. But sadly, our relationships do not work that way. They follow the same principle as growing a plant: constant care is required so that one day, it blooms. There are no short cuts. It's all in our small but consistent gestures. The most widely underestimated quality that can help us improve our relationships is forgiveness.'

'If only forgiving someone was as easy as changing television channels,' Harry said. 'There is always a part of me that cannot forget the bad things people have done to me. It becomes hard to trust them after a while.'

'Forgiveness is hard to theorize. It is a bit like salt: you know only when it's missing!' I laughed. Going by Harry's reaction I thought the joke was funnier in my head. 'Forgiveness warms the heart and cools the sting. It is a choice that each of us has to make for ourselves to save our relationships and achieve peace of mind. There are a few things we should remember, in practising forgiveness.'

Look beyond the Situation

The ancient histories of the East are not only exciting to read, but teach us practical moral lessons. In fact, most of the principles I've applied to my life are based either on these sacred texts or on the experiences of people who live by them! One such text is the *Ramayana*. It tells the tale of Prince Rama, who was famously exiled to a distant forest for fourteen years because of the selfish political motivations of his stepmother, Kaikeyi. He did not go alone, however. His dear wife, Sita, and loyal brother, Laxman, willingly accompanied him, as he gave up the throne.

One day, a few years into their journey, Sita saw an unusual yet radiant golden deer frolicking about. Enchanted by its beauty, she pleaded with Rama to capture it for her. Happy to do so, Rama set off to capture it but left Laxman with strict instructions to guard Sita while he was away. Who knew what lurked among the trees!

It was then that a voice echoed in the forest, 'Sita, help me!' The silence of the forest consumed it. 'Laxman, please, somebody help me!' the voice called out a second time. Laxman and Sita both looked perplexed.

Intuitively, a telepathic understanding was exchanged between them: *That sounds like Rama's voice, but he has never called for help like this before.* Little did they know the golden deer that Rama was chasing was the demon Maricha in disguise. Could the valiant warrior Rama really be in trouble?

'Laxman, go and save him. You must help your brother,' Sita commanded Laxman but to no avail. He knew Rama would be fine—he had just defeated thousands of demons in the forest without breaking a sweat. What could a deer do to harm him? 'It is your duty to go!' Sita panicked. Just the thought of one's beloved being in some sort of danger can bring an outpouring of emotion within the lover.

'My brother can protect himself,' Laxman said, gazing into the darkness, as snakes slithered and various winged creatures flew past. 'But you cannot. My duty is to protect you. Rama would never forgive me if I left you here, vulnerable to whatever lurks in the darkness.'

Some of us who are familiar with this story know the dangers that lurked in the darkness. Laxman paced up and down, like a palace guard. But this was no palace—it was a straw hut, held together by damp earth. Anyone could have been loitering in such a place.

'We are in the middle of nowhere,' Sita argued. 'I order you, I command you, I beg of you to go and save your brother. I have a feeling that he is in real danger.' They say pulling rank is the last refuge in an argument, but people say anything when they are distressed. A few minutes passed in silence.

'Help me, please! Someone!' came another shout from the distance.

'That is your brother calling to us for help! How can you do nothing?' Sita screamed. 'I see. Now that Rama is out of the picture, you think you can have me for yourself. You want the kingdom all to yourself.' Sita knew that was not true and that Laxman would have done anything for Rama, but she wanted a reaction. Laxman hung his head in sorrow, fixing his gaze upon the sand by his feet. What an accusation for him to face from someone he had dedicated his whole life in service to; his heart was crushed. 'Please go and save your brother,' Sita pleaded again, more gently this time.

Laxman made sure that his sister-in-law was safe and then ran into the forest in pursuit of Rama.

This episode is particularly powerful in the context of forgiveness. Sita had pierced and caused injury to Laxman's heart with the arrows of her harsh words. In our lives, we may find that we are cast as both Sita and Laxman. Sometimes we are the ones stringing the bow, and at other times, we are the ones under fire. But it's important to note an unbiased perspective.

What Sita said was factually wrong, and it was insensitive of her to have made such accusations against her brother-in-law. However, if we look past the situation, that is, if we look past *what* was said, we might be able to understand *why* it was said. Sita was going through a personal turmoil. Her emotions were flying about as she speculated on the kind of pain her beloved husband might have been going through. We have all been in situations where our intellect is clouded by our emotions. At those times, we say anything and everything for our own peace of mind. Although a moment of patience in a moment of anger can save us a thousand moments of regret in the future, usually when we are suffering intensely, we cannot help but let our minds run amok. For our own growth, we should maintain equipoise in testing times. When someone hurts us, we should try to look beyond the situation and think: 'How are they suffering? What are they feeling, to say such a thing? Is there some deeper chaos that is occurring in their life for them to say these words to me?' It's not about supporting the hurtful comments made by others—it is about seeing what they are going through to be making them. This is empathy, an essential component of forgiveness.

Separate the Episode from the Person

It is said, 'Sticks and stones may break my bones, but words will never hurt me.' This could not be further from the truth. Physical violence is inflicted with weapons, but emotional violence is inflicted with words; words can leave invisible scars that can take years, or even lifetimes, to heal.

Let me take your mind back to Nepal, to the foothills of the Himalayas and to the story of my closest friend who had spoken harshly to me in front of our community members. What happened in my room thereafter is relevant here—I was able to move from anger to forgiveness because I remembered to separate the episode from the person. Of course, I must mention that this principle is not applicable in all situations—especially those of social justice, which I will discuss later—but in our personal interactions, for the most part, it works wonders.

When I fail at something—whether it's an exam or a relationship—I may think that I am a failure. But just because I failed one time or even more than once in my life, does that really make the whole of *me* a failure? Similarly, just because someone may, on a rare occasion, have failed us, should we treat that person like a failure? Should we not see that lapse as an independent event? Everyone is going through challenges concealed from the public eye, and we need the lens of empathy to be able to see that.

This is not to say that we should tolerate abuse or not do the sensible thing and correct someone when they are wrong, but in order to practise forgiveness, we have to learn to separate the incident from the person. Disconnecting the person from the problem starts with the language we use to describe the incident:

- Saying 'it is *my* problem' causes us to feel guilty, and over time, one may develop an inferiority complex. We may begin to think that we are not tough enough to deal with situations and thus we may become morose over issues.

- Saying 'it is *your* problem' causes us to feel angry. How many times have we pointed our index finger at someone and used the words, 'It's *your* problem, not mine.'? I have never seen anyone say those words in a peaceful state of mind. Blaming the other person only leads to a spiral of anger.
- Saying 'it is *the* problem' separates the problem from the persons involved. Not only does this separation empower us to forgive the person, it also helps us to effectively deal with the problem.

Higher Purpose

After setting the groundwork for forgiveness, I now felt that Harry was ready to hear the story I had promised to tell him. In my opinion, the couple in my story was in a far worse situation than Harry and Lalita. However, it is hard to compare people's sufferings. That's why I avoid doing so. Like many of my other stories, the incident this one is based on also took place during my travels.

I travel so often that sometimes I give a morning talk in Chennai, and by the evening, I'm speaking in Kolkata. One day I am in California, and the next, I'm in Cape Town. It's only natural that I feel connected to so many different communities, meeting a variety of people from around the globe. One community, which I frequently travel to but will not mention here to protect all those involved in the incident, is where this story starts.

I had just finishing unpacking. I would be staying in this room for a week, which was an age for me. I usually live out of my suitcase because, like a shepherd, I am always searching for new lands to spread my message of positivity. I sat down cross-legged and was just about to start with my evening meditation when a man burst into my room, letting his tears fall to the wooden floor. Alarmed at his overflowing emotion, I shot up immediately, my knees clicking.

'She's cheating on me!' he exclaimed. I shut the door to my room and closed the blinds. My instinct was to pour him some herbal tea. My mother always used to say that when someone is upset, the warmth of herbal tea and a friend's words can help to heal them. He sat on the floor with me. 'She's cheating on me . . .' he said again, in between sips of his camomile beverage.

I had been friends with this man for over twenty years. In fact, I had attended an event as part of his wedding ceremony, counselled his family through thick and thin, but I had never expected him to say something like this. He was an engineer, had one seventeen-year-old son who was expected to follow in his father's footsteps, and lived in a three-bedroom apartment—an ordinary gentleman, with an ordinary job, caught in this extraordinary situation.

'What happened?' I asked as I held his hands. His tear-filled eyes, quivering like the air in a heatwave, looked back into mine.

'Yesterday, I was checking my wife's phone to get the address for a wedding function we were supposed to attend later in the evening and I saw multiple notifications from a man.' He mentioned who the man was—he was a senior member of their community, and held an important position of leadership. 'I thought nothing of it at first; he contacts many people to invite them to work with him. But as I scrolled down and looked through the messages he was sending my wife . . . they were not innocent. I can't even tell you what I read. And she had replied similarly.' He let his tears drop into his tea, which was now lukewarm. With his upper lip quivering, he said: 'At that moment, my wife walked in and saw me on her phone. From the look in my eyes she knew that I knew.'

'"What's this all about?" I asked her directly without hesitation. I had decided to communicate and clarify what was going on, without jumping to conclusions straight away. My wife paused for a moment and then came towards me. She said, "I have been messaging him for a few weeks now. I'm sorry; I don't know what came over me. It started out innocently. He needed help with some work, but then it led to more."'

One very admirable thing about his wife is that she has always been down-to-earth and honest.

He continued, 'I asked her, "Have you met and—" but she interrupted me, saying, "No, of course not. We've never met."'

This meant that they had never had a physical relationship, but even so, I could tell that this incident had left an emotional scar on this man. Sometimes the deepest wounds are inflicted by people who are closest to us. How could he trust her after this? How could he forgive her? Had she done this before? I could see that these were the thoughts that were tormenting his mind.

I also knew the man his wife had been talking to. After this incident, he was asked to step down from his position because not only does a leader have to pave the path for a community, he has to walk along it too. He did confirm that he had never had a physical relationship with this man's wife.

'What shall I do about the situation?' the man asked me. I poured him a second cup of herbal tea. 'How can I trust her again?'

That dangerous question again: *What shall I do?* I thought. I am no one's guru. Everyone must make their own choices; nobody should *tell* us what to do, but good advice greatly helps us in our growth. With that in mind I asked, 'Do you love your wife?'

'Without a doubt,' he said.

'You should always keep that in mind when making any decisions. But right now, you only have two choices.' He calmed down a little. 'Do you want to choose justice or do you want to choose forgiveness? Either is fine, but you have to make the choice—justice may cost you your marriage and this news may go public, ruining many lives. And that's fine, if justice is what you need. People have their own capacity for what is acceptable to them and what is not.'

He started to focus on his priorities.

'I can't leave her. We have a seventeen-year-old son who will be distraught. Nothing like this has happened in the past in our family. I am really sad because I thought our bond was stronger than this . . .'

'Then you have to forgive. Maybe this is just circumstantial. Are you willing to give her another chance?'

'How can I forgive? I'll only think about what she did to me every time I look at her,' he said.

'Forgiveness means to take note of the higher purpose. Weren't you telling me during my visit last year that she is the best mother to your son and how she has given him so much affection, dedication and love? Focus on the higher purpose that brought you together. It would shatter your son if you decided to divorce now. Besides, if she is willing to make amends, give forgiveness a chance. Although infidelity is the hardest thing to forgive, it is no match for a relationship that is driven by a higher purpose. Do we want to be right or harmonize for a higher purpose?'

'It will take time to make this decision,' he said.

I poured him a third cup. *Third time's a charm!* I thought to myself.

'Take as much time as you need. Time heals, and with the right association and guidance, time brings clarity. Relationships are tested during difficult times. To accept someone when everything is going right is easy. But when things are falling apart around you and you stick together, that's the test of a relationship. Love is when we have every reason to break up but we do not.'

We spoke for some time on the issue before I introduced another concept to him—the difference between forgiveness and justice.

Justice

Some spiritual leaders would advise us to always forgive, regardless of the situation. Although that sounds like the most peaceful approach, it can end up doing more harm than good sometimes.

Sexual violence has long been a serious and widespread problem all over the world, and the perpetrators can sometimes even go unpunished. In December 2012, I remember being horrified as I read reports about a twenty-three-year-old woman who had been brutally raped for several hours and then dumped by six young men in New Delhi, India. In the days following the attack, newspaper reports elaborated on the gruesome nature of the rape. She did not survive. It was an incident that shocked the entire nation, and provoked widespread international condemnation for the treatment of women in India. I was not surprised by the protests that happened all over the country. They wanted justice for the young lady and reform in the courts so that women feel protected.

The question is: Should we have forgiven the men who raped the twenty-three-year-old physiotherapy student? In the ancient classic the *Bhagavad Gita*, Arjuna asks Sri Krishna about a similar dilemma of forgiveness. War had come to Hastinapur, which is modern-day New Delhi. Arjuna's cousins had brought tyranny and immorality to the kingdom, and after months of peace negotiations, the only solution left was war. This occurred 5,000 years ago. There were codes of conduct that were followed diligently; war was only fought between armies, not civilians.

Throughout the *Bhagavad Gita*, Arjuna tries to convince Sri Krishna that the best thing to do is not to fight. He is a pacifist. 'Why partake in bloodshed when you can retreat? Surely it is better to forgive those who perform such transgressions?' Arjuna argues. But Sri Krishna whole-heartedly disagrees with his cousin and shares the wisdom of social justice.

On a personal level, we can forgive those who hurt us. That is a personal choice, available to all of us. However, on a societal level, such heinous crimes, if left unpunished, can create havoc. The social repercussions of allowing those who break the law to go free are devastating. Therefore, Sri Krishna encouraged Arjuna to lift his bow, because in this case fighting was the right thing to do.

Similarly, the men who perform the criminal act of rape should face the full force of justice, as casual actions in the name of forgiveness do nothing to help society progress. If these criminals are not detained and punished, can you imagine the message it will send out? The principle of forgiveness and the principle of social justice go hand-in-hand; it takes wisdom and introspection to know how they are to be used.

It had been an intense few minutes in the car with Harry. The concept of forgiveness is far from light. It is complicated and hard to understand, but I could see that he was trying to accept it. I explained, 'The topic of relationships has spiritual roots. If we can understand how to relate to people on a spiritual level, then we can transcend our dividing differences.'

Monk Mindset:

- Forgiveness is a deep and often obscure value to understand.
- The principles we should know about forgiveness are:
  - o Look beyond the situation: If we are hurt by someone's words, try to understand why they spoke them. When people act harshly towards us, most of the time they are suffering too. This is empathy.
  - o Separate the episode from the person: Rather than being affected by the emotion of guilt by saying, 'I am wrong,' or anger by saying, 'You are wrong,' we should separate the *I* or the *You* and deal with the wrong.
  - o Higher purpose: Can we forgive based on a higher principle? For example, in my story, the husband forgave the wife because he loved her, and they had a duty to their community and son. If chosen, this approach takes support and time and is not something that happens overnight.
  - o Justice: On a personal level, we can forgive the person who may have wronged us, but on a societal level, there should be strict justice to create an orderly society. No one should be able to break the law and get away with it in the name of forgiveness.

Note: To help you reflect on forgiving someone in your own life, please complete the exercise in Appendix 1 (Forgiveness Worksheet).

TWELVE

Association Matters

Our relationships are stronger when they contain a spiritual component. There are three different ways to become good friends with someone.

It is hard to imagine a life without relationships. The principle of relationships is an inherent universal one that guides our lives. What would life be if we did not have others to share it with? Therefore, we must learn how to do it correctly. Although this skill is seldom taught in schools, it has been documented in ancient spiritual texts for thousands of years. Your association, called sanga in Sanskrit, is crucial to your success, in this world and beyond.

Our association can uplift or depress us to the lowest levels. When I talk about association in this context, I do not mean general interactions. In our day-to-day life, all of us will have to interact with people who may not necessarily be the best influence on us. Yet, we will have to do the needful and such interactions are simply neutral dealings hardly causing us any harm. Association is beyond our neutral 'hi-hello dealings'— it has to do with the level of intimacy we share with others.

One ancient text on relationships describes six exchanges that can create intimacy in personal dealings:

> *dadāti pratigṛhṇāti*
> *guhyam ākhyāti pṛcchati*
> *bhuṅkte bhojayate caiva*
> *ṣaḍ-vidhaṁ prīti-lakṣaṇam*

Offering gifts and accepting gifts, opening one's mind and inquiring in confidence, sharing food and receiving food are the six exchanges that develop loving relationships.

We can broadly divide these into three different principles:

The first principle—*dadāti pratigṛhṇāti*—means giving and receiving. Intimacy in our association begins with giving and receiving. For example, we may allow someone to use our car for the day or invite them to stay at our house, or in the modern day, share something even more valuable, like our Wi-Fi password! And the person may in turn reciprocate and return the favour in the future. We do not exchange our things and facilities with just anyone we meet. Such an exchange occurs only with people who we are intimate with or with those who we want to be intimate with. It is the extra effort that we put into these general interactions that develops intimacy.

The second principle—*bhuṅkte bhojayate caiva*—which means 'exchange of food with each other', takes our association to the next level. 'Why don't you come to my house for lunch this afternoon?' we may say. In India, there is a very popular coffee outlet and their tag line is 'A lot can happen over coffee'. This is true—a lot does happen over the sharing of food. There is a deep emotional bonding that happens when we break bread together. The intimacy of our connection grows deeper from just sharing things, to sharing meals. Over meals and those light moments, a lot of our heart is shared, which brings us to principle three.

The third principle—*guhyam ākhyāti pṛcchati*—means we start revealing our heart in confidence and listening to the other person's revelations in confidence. When someone pours out their heart to us, we are not only understanding their point of view but subconsciously also being influenced by their values and beliefs.

Thus, intimate association is about interactions that go beyond doing the needful; beginning with sharing things, moving on to sharing food and, finally, sharing thoughts, values and beliefs.

Traffic was moving slowly through Mumbai, but at least we were still moving. We were just approaching the Haji Ali Dargah, a beautiful place of worship built into the bay. You could see people in the distance scurrying across the bridge that leads to the white marble building. After the mosque came the Haji Ali Chowk or crossroads. We were there physically, but I also felt that we were there metaphorically. Harry was at a crossroads in his life, questioning the decisions he had made in his relationships. It is natural to feel that way because it is the nature of the world to make you feel unsettled.

Our conversation was disturbed by Harry's phone vibrating in the door-pocket of the car. Not wanting to distract himself, he declined the call without seeing who it was.

'You can take the call, if you like,' I said.

'Are you sure?' he replied.

I nodded. He checked his call register.

'Oh, it was my wife calling . . . After all that we have discussed, maybe I should call her back,' he said, embarrassed.

'Definitely,' I said and smiled.

He pressed the number, lodged his phone between his ear and shoulder and placed both his hands on the steering wheel again.

'Hello? Are you there?' he repeated many times.

'Hi . . . I'm going to . . . I'm okay . . . should be home soon . . . with your mother,' a voice on the other side repeated loud enough for me to overhear without intending to do so.

'The signal is bad,' Harry said to me. 'She's off somewhere. I couldn't make out where, but she's with Mum. Should be okay.'

I thought nothing of it at the time, but as it turned out she was off to somewhere very important. But we were not to know that until much later.

'Now, where were we?' Harry quickly changed the subject. 'We were talking about relationships and the interactions we have with people. With my wife, I know that I have a lot to do, but most of the stress that I bring home is from work. In a corporate environment, the dynamics are odd. I must cooperate with my colleagues, but at the same time I want to get ahead. How do I deal with my interactions at work?'

I told him, 'Fun fact: I know that you spend more than forty hours a week at work, but let's say that on average a person spends forty hours working between the ages of twenty and sixty-five, and gets two weeks of holiday a year. In that time, they will have worked a total of 90,000 hours. That's a lot of time, so we better learn how to best utilize it in the right way.' It was also time to explain the third wheel of life.

Monk Mindset:

- Our association is powerful: it can uplift us or bring us down.
- General interactions are dealings meant to do the needful and are simply neutral.
- Intimate dealings are built through the exchange of things, food, thoughts, values and belief systems. Our lifestyle is affected more by another person's value systems than their habits.

WHEEL 3
WORK LIFE

THIRTEEN

Competition Crossroads

At work we tend to compare and compete with others, instead of comparing and competing with ourselves.

We were edging closer to the ashram, where I was now over two hours late for my meeting. There was no point in panicking; controlling the traffic was beyond my influence. 'Look at the motorbikes and cars and cab drivers. Getting stuck in traffic can make people really angry,' I said over a cacophony of hooting and swearing by other drivers around us. 'Everyone wants to get ahead of each other, and when they cannot, they get angry.'

'It is like my workplace,' Harry intervened. 'As I said, I need to be friendly with people at my workplace, because we need to complete projects together, but there is also this air of competition. How can I get rid of that?' He paused for a moment to think. 'Actually, I cannot help but compete. If I don't do that then I will never get the promotion I want. I am not volunteering for my company, I have bills to pay!' He laughed.

'I understand your dilemma. This issue is not just unique to the working world. It's found in all spheres of life, whether it is between students, professionals, couples or even monks! Competition is a mindset that we have to redefine.'

I began explaining to Harry:

'Many years ago, when I was in college, I remember auditioning to sing at our annual social gathering. It wasn't a big role, but I had been encouraged by my friends to take part as they felt I had a good voice. I walked out on to the stage with the spotlight glaring down on me and three judges ready to give me a score. I heard rumours that I was likely to get the part, but I didn't look too much into it. The microphone was at the centre of the stage. I held it and sang the hit Bollywood song of that summer. Remember, at that point I wasn't a monk yet! The music faded in from the speakers and I started singing.

'"Stop, stop, stop . . ." one of the engineering professors, who was also a judge, said, raising his hand. "Do you have something stuck in your throat? Have some water and start again."

'I was confused, my throat was fine, but I sipped some water to make sure that I wasn't missing anything. The music faded in again. I sang half the song, but they stopped me halfway with disappointed looks on their faces.

'*It just wasn't my day today*, I thought, but I had tried my best. A little disheartened, I returned home ready to focus on studying again. It was only a week later that I found out what had really happened.

'The sound engineer who controlled my microphone came up to me in the college bathroom and said, "I felt really bad that you couldn't get the part last week."

"'Why do you have to feel bad?" I asked, washing away the soap from my hands. I hardly knew this person.

"'Well . . . the person who got the part paid me to adjust the setting so that your audition sounded terrible. It's been playing on my conscience all week," he said, looking at the floor.

"'What?" I said in shock.

"'I'm sorry. If you want, I can report this to the judges and see what can be done . . ." he said, grovelling.

"'No, no, it's all right. I haven't got the time anyway. But thanks for telling me," I said as I dried my hands with paper towels. He then walked out of the bathroom.

'I was in disbelief. Why would someone sabotage my audition? It wasn't anything significant. There were no monetary rewards, trophies or extra marks. Since studying was my main priority, I decided not to take it up with the judges nor to confront the boy who had got the part. Having witnessed the ugly side of his competitive nature, I did become more suspicious of him.

'*What could have driven him to be so competitive?* I thought as I walked back into the classroom.

Jealousy or Envy

One reason I thought of was that he was, possibly, envious of me. When one harbours ill feelings towards others wanting to be like them or better than them but does not act on those feelings, it is called jealousy. Although the feeling eats one up from the inside, one still has the self-control to not harm the other person. However, when one does act on those feelings, jealousy turns into envy. And envy is the root cause of being competitive with others in a way where one does not mind going to any extent to take their place.

Uncontrolled Ambition

Another reason I could think of was that people want to be the best, sometimes at any cost. When there are limited resources and many takers, competition is natural. This is found in all domains of life, from music to sport and even among other species. Competition is a tendency that occurs in nearly every ecosystem in nature.

'But human beings are not just another species. They have the ability to cooperate and subscribe to higher values such as harmony, loyalty and trust. Just as within natural ecosystems competition is greater within the same species, within humans competition is fierce within the same company or the same field of action. We compete with people who have the same skills or outlook in life as us. An engineer competes with another engineer, a musician with another musician and a doctor with another doctor. When another person's skills have no bearing on our life, we rarely feel threatened. But if someone can outperform us by doing better in what we aspire to do, the base tendencies of competition can settle in.

Sports

Every sport has an element of competition to it and there is a joy in pushing yourself to the limit. But when the stakes are high, the prestige and prize of winning may completely overshadow the ethic of 'doing your best', and some players may even play dirty to win. Whether it is over-exaggerating injuries in a football tournament or tampering with the ball to make it swing more in flight in a cricket match, players have been seen putting their hard-earned reputation and even their sports career on the line simply for some cheap, short-term gains.

Business

Companies will almost always compete to grab the biggest market share and be the best in the industry, unless they have a monopoly in a particular sector. After all, a capitalist society is based on the premise of increasing profits and having more for oneself. And that's fine, as long as such competition is driven by sheer ambition. But when ambition crosses the line of ethics and turns into greed, even reputed businesses can get involved with scandals as they vie for the largest piece of the pie.

Politics

Rather than contesting an election based on merit, politicians may sometimes be seen spreading lies to sway voters, suppressing voters on polling days, threatening opponents or even assassinating a candidate! And the root cause is unethical competition.

Workplace

Although competition in the arena of sports, business or politics may be a distant reality for many, workplace politics and competition is something they may have very closely experienced. Gossip, back-stabbing, spreading lies and not cooperating with co-workers on purpose can be forms of unhealthy competition to get to the top. But if you want to grow you have to compete.

Healthy Competition

'The only difference is who are you competing with,' I added. 'People with a closed mindset want to grow by beating others in their field. Open-minded people, on the other hand, grow by developing themselves. They know that nobody is their competition. They are their own competition. Every day they keep striving to become better versions of themselves, even if the growth is only a tiny fragment. They feel uncomfortable if they remain the same as they were yesterday. The actor Matthew McConaughey spoke about this principle in his 2014 Oscar acceptance speech.'

'Oh, yes. I have seen it on YouTube,' Harry replied.

Since the car was still at a halt, I pulled out my phone and played the short video.

The words of the American actor echoed around the car: 'And to my hero. That's who I chase. Now when I was fifteen years old, I had a very important person in my life come to me and say, "Who's your hero?" And I said, "I don't know, I gotta think about that. Give me a couple of weeks." I come back two weeks later, this person comes up and says, "Who's your hero?" I said, "I thought about it. You know who it is? It's me in ten years." So I turned twenty-five. Ten years later, that same person comes to me and says, "So, are you a hero?" And

I was like, "Not even close. No, no, no." She said, "Why?" I said, "Because my hero's me at thirty-five." So, you see, every day, every week, every month and every year of my life, my hero's always ten years away. I'm never gonna be my hero. I'm not gonna attain that. I know I'm not, and that's just fine with me because that keeps me with somebody to keep on chasing.'

As the video ended, I put my phone back in my pocket and shared my reflection, 'We should imbibe this thought pattern of self-competition, rather than feeling insecure about others going ahead. We should be striving to do our very best to realize our dreams about our future selves. Not only will this attitude keep our mind free from envy and insecurity but it will also help us reach our fullest potential, bringing immense success and a deep sense of satisfaction.'

A young boy learning the traditional Kathak dance was regularly missing his steps and stumbling during practice. Frustrated, he came to his teacher and asked, 'When will I be able to dance finely like your other students? When will I be able to keep up with the beats and perform every move with grace?'

The teacher replied, 'When you stop looking at your fellow students during the practice. Remember, you're not in competition with them. You're in competition with yourself. Your goal is to simply be better than you were yesterday, not better than the other boys and girls in the class.'

Whether in dancing, playing a sport, in business or anything in life, this ideology brings self-excellence. And we see this ideology in play at Apple Inc.

Only if you lived in a cave somewhere in the Gobi Desert would you not know that Apple is one of the most successful companies of the modern era. Have you ever bought an iPhone from an Apple Store on the day of its launch? You're greeted by hundreds of staff, all in matching uniforms, who clap and cheer loudly as you purchase their newest product. Although I have never seen this, my friends tell me it's like a party. People become hysterical. But what is it that makes Apple so innovative that people keep coming back to them? The answer is found in the culture given by their leadership.

The late Steve Jobs, the founder of Apple, believed that competing with others was a distraction from your own inner creativity. To not strive for originality would have been disastrous for Apple. If we compare ourselves with others too much, we succumb to ordinariness. We can start blindly imitating others and even lose our essence. In the worst-case scenario, we becoming boring! Steve Jobs was notorious for paying careful attention to detail in all his products. He wanted to change the world, not just copy the next best company to increase his stock price. He wanted to express himself fully, not just follow the expressions of others. He wanted to compare himself to what he had done in the past, not just with Bill Gates!

'So are you trying to say that comparison with others is always bad?' Harry interrupted.

'No,' I replied. 'If we do have to compare ourselves with others, we should compare positive attitudes. That person's attitude to tirelessly keep working or grinding at their skills is inspiring. I want that same attitude. Let me learn from them and in turn help them in any way I can. Let us mutually grow. That is how an open-minded person thinks.'

'That sounds great. But when competitive people around you engage in dirty politics to drag you down and grab the deal, should you just keep quiet and continue to work on?' Harry objected.

'There will always be those who play dirty politics at the workplace,' I replied. 'This seems to be in every office, like moisture in the air. Wherever there are human beings, you will find two types of people: those who work in honest ways, living with integrity, and those who don't. Of course, this is a generalization. Nobody has a perfect moral compass, neither is anyone completely morally bankrupt. Even if you leave your job to join another company, there will be people engaging in politics there as well. It may be a little less or a little more, and may be of a different flavour. However, we must learn how to manage demanding situations at the workplace in a clean way. There are a few books written by experienced professionals that explain, in great detail, the subject of dealing with workplace politics. I highly recommend that you read one of those books. The bottom line, however, is, rather than being political, it is better to constantly work hard on self-improvement to achieve excellence. When it is impossible to stay surrounded by the negativity of bosses and colleagues, it is better to move on. Only if you have another work option, of course.'

Monk Mindset:

- There are two causes of unhealthy competition, being envious of someone or uncontrolled ambition.
- We compete with people who have the same skills or outlook in life as us. When another person's skills have no bearing on our life, we rarely feel threatened.
- Competition is found in all spheres of life. Some examples include sports, business, politics and the workplace.
- Healthy competition is about competing with ourselves rather than others to become a better version of ourselves.
- There will always be workplace politics but we should learn how to manage it in a clean way.

FOURTEEN

Self-Discovery

To find your purpose in life, you must go on a journey of self-discovery.

Harry thanked me for the insights. Wanting to take the conversation further, he asked, 'What do you think is the key element needed for self-improvement and competition with oneself?'

'If there is one thing that I think is the foundation of growth, it is understanding who you are. You can only compete with yourself if you have a clear idea of your potential, your capacities and certainly your limitations,' I replied.

Harry listened with great interest as I elaborated the concept further.

Understanding Ourselves

We have to understand ourselves to be able to compete with ourselves. What are our tendencies? What do we like? What do we not like? Where do we want to be in the future? These are only a few preliminary questions we need to answer to succeed. And this process of inquiry begins our journey of self-discovery.

I used to always wonder why one would put in so much effort using fancy paper, bows and ribbons to wrap a gift. Why can we not just give the gift upfront to the person who we want to express our love for? I came to the conclusion that if we offer a gift to someone without wrapping it, there is no element of excitement involved. Concealing a gift creates suspense, and when it is opened there is excitement and thus great joy. Not only does the person who receives the gift feel happy but so does the one who gives it.

In the same way, everyone has been gifted with special talents and skills. Every individual has something unique in them. If God were to reveal that talent to us straight away, from the very day we were born, there would be no excitement in our journey. God covers our talent, skills and potential only so that we have the chance to *discover* it. And in the process of doing so, in trying to figure out what we want to do with our lives, there is a tremendous sense of satisfaction. Self-discovery is not a one-time event but an ongoing evolution, and as life goes on we discover how much we are capable of achieving.

Did you ever play 'pass the parcel' as a child? A classic at birthday parties, the game is centred around a prize wrapped up in a large number of gift wrappers. Between each layer of wrapping there is a smaller gift. As the music starts playing, the parcel is passed around a group of people, in anticipation of the music stopping. When it does, the person who now has the parcel in their hand removes one layer of wrapping paper and claims the small prize. The same process continues until the penultimate wrapper, when all the small prizes are gone and finally the main prize is revealed to the one who holds and unwraps the last layer.

Now, what has this children's game got to do with understanding ourselves? We need to unwrap multiple layers before we can actually discover our true potential. The further we delve towards realizing our potential, the more layers we start to uncover, and with every layer we come across smaller gifts that were hidden within us. We do not have to wait to experience happiness until all the layers are taken off and the large gift—our true potential—is revealed to us. The journey itself is very exciting and brings deep satisfaction. When I think about this, it reminds me about the story of my young friend Sairaj.

Blueberry Cheesecake

On a surprisingly cool evening in Mumbai, I was invited to a Gujarati family's home for dinner. They had been pleading with me to come for months, and Gujarati mothers can be very persuasive. So on their fifth invitation, I obliged.

Both parents in the household were working professionals. They were as busy as I was, but I noticed they always took time out for two things: spirituality and their son, Sairaj.

You can imagine the spread of delicious Gujarati items on offer. From dhokla to undhiyu, and from khandvi to shrikhand, they had not spared any efforts. As I sat down, I enquired about Sairaj, who had just completed his tenth-grade exams.

'He should be down in a moment,' the father said. 'He is so excited to see you.'

'I heard he did very well in his exams,' I said.

'Yes, he works very hard,' the mother said, as she told me his marks. At that very moment, Sairaj walked into the room. He greeted me with a big hug and sat next to me at the dinner table.

'Your mother was telling me that you got 93 per cent marks this year and that you did exceptionally well in mathematics and science!' I said.

Sairaj blushed. He was humble despite his academic achievements.

'Thank you! I'm excited for the next year,' he said energetically.

'What stream have you chosen for the next year?' I asked as Sairaj's father forced more dhokla on to my plate.

In India, children usually choose streams of subjects depending on their marks. Typically, children with very good marks choose engineering or medicine. I expected Sairaj would follow.

Sairaj looked at his father and then looked down. 'I am choosing commerce,' he said. The expressions on his parents' faces changed. Why had he chosen commerce instead of the other streams, when he was capable of doing well at them? Stereotypically, commerce did not have as much scope in India as the other subjects did.

'That's great,' I replied after a moment. I always try to encourage people's decisions and dreams. 'What will you do in university, then?' I asked.

At that moment, Sairaj's mother brought out a blueberry cheesecake on a crystal plate.

'Many people do not know this but the base of the blueberry cheesecake, which is made from graham cracker crumbs, sugar and butter, has to be baked at a high temperature for *one* hour!' Sairaj said.

That was an odd change of subject for a sixteen-year-old boy, I thought.

'You then have to chill it for another hour so it stays firm like it is on the plate,' Sairaj said, and then went on to describe the chocolate mousse that was setting in the fridge, and then shifted to savoury snacks like the dhokla and khandvi on the table. When he was doing this, you should have seen the expressions on his parents' faces. Can you imagine what they must have been thinking?

'I want to get into a career of hospitality and catering, after I finish commerce,' Sairaj said, after a short while. The mood in the room changed again, with his parents' faces also changing. Their expressions were not what one would expect—they were of great joy and happiness, all through!

'I know what Sairaj wants to do with his life is not conventional. I told him he might want to take after his mother and that medicine might suit him better. However, he refused and kept cooking and cooking and cooking,' his father said, elated. 'I couldn't be happier, because he has found his passion in life, and I get to eat delicious desserts after work!' He laughed.

'Naturally, we were concerned that being a chef won't make him as much money, but he loves what he does and he is good at it. India is a growing country with so much scope for being an entrepreneur,' his mother added while cutting me a slice of cheesecake that was clearly too big for my stomach.

'I am going to help him with the business side,' his father said, beaming.

'It seems as though you have it all figured out,' I said, excited by the unique future that was ahead of Sairaj. I would not be surprised if this boy ended up opening a chain of five-star restaurants all over the world!

On the way back to the ashram after dinner, I thought to myself that if someone chooses what they love to do, there is no stress in their life. As they say, 'If you do what you love, you will never have to work a day in your life.' However, in reality, the majority of people are doing what they do not love to do, day in and day out.

Ikigai

Just like Sairaj, we all need to find purpose, which has been linked with longer and happier lives. There are many psychological models that can aid us on our path to living fulfilling lives, one of which is the concept of *ikigai*.

Ikigai has no direct English translation, but is understood to mean 'a reason to live' or having purpose in life. It comes from Japan, the country with the highest number of the most elderly people in the world. The island of Okinawa has an average male life expectancy of seventy-eight and an average female life expectancy of eighty-six!

According to Akihiro Hasegawa, a clinical psychologist from Toyo Eiwa University, the word *gai* originates from the word *kai*, which translates as shell. He says that in the Heian period (794–1185) shells were considered extremely valuable. Therefore, gai now means to have 'value in living'.

According to this concept, to find purpose in life, you have to answer four questions, just as Sairaj and his family did subconsciously:

- What do you love?
- What are you good at?
- What does the world need?
- What can you get paid for?

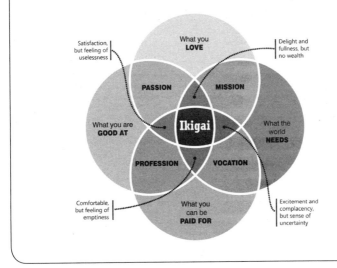

Finding balance between the four areas may be the route to having a life that one looks forward to living. Not everybody's purpose will appear to have an impact on the course of the world at first—it could be something as simple as Sairaj's was.

'However, not everyone is as young as Sairaj,' Harry laughed as we were edging closer to more familiar parts of Mumbai. We had just passed some expensive designer shops. 'If you have a lifestyle that is linked to wearing such expensive clothes,' Harry pointed to the displays in the window, 'then it is hard to change your existing career and do what you love. At one point, I wanted to work with nature, as a conservationist to protect the environment, but that would not pay well,' he confessed.

'You do not need to give up everything or make dramatic changes to start living your purpose. Your purpose does not necessarily mean your job either,' I replied.

'So then what do I do? I do not have any children yet, so I know that I can make time,' Harry added.

'You have to act on two things. The first is, love what you have to do. We all have to pay bills, maintain our lifestyle and work in the jobs we are already in. For most people, this work that we may not be passionate about is around 80 per cent of our lives. Therefore, we might as well start loving it! Which parts of your job do you love? Focus on those parts.'

'I suppose I like working with other colleagues on client projects,' he said.

'Then try and focus on that,' I said. 'The second thing is, make time in life for what you love to do. Start adding conservation and the environment into your life. Explore India over weekends! Research which forests or areas need help and how best you can help!' I said passionately. I did not know much about helping the environment, but he understood my point. 'We tend to waste our time off work by doing mundane things that bring us no satisfaction: window-shopping, eating out at the same places, and so on. There is a whole world out there to explore, and many people who feel the same way. We have to take a calculated risk to start adding what we truly love to do, our ikigai, into our lives. Maybe one day what we love to do and what pays the bills can be the same if we really work on ourselves!'

Monk Mindset:

- We should understand ourselves to know what is meaningful to us, and what we want to devote our time to. This can be done by understanding our purpose, which takes dedication and patience.
- Discovering our purpose is exciting, just as opening a gift gives the feeling of anticipation and joy. Reaching our purpose in life is a journey, not an event.
- The Japanese have a model called ikigai or a 'reason to live', which is composed of four traits we need to understand: What do we love? What are we good at? What does the world need? What can we be paid for? Sairaj and his family discovered that for him early on in his life.
- If we are older and have not yet figured out our purpose, we can follow the principle: love what we have to do and do what we love to do.

Note: To help you find your ikigai, you can complete an exercise in Appendix 2 (Ikigai Worksheet).

FIFTEEN

Decoding Spirituality at Work

This chapter clears the many misconceptions about spirituality: that spiritualists are not ambitious, that spiritualists will get walked over at the workplace because of their values and that we should not aspire to the nicer things in life.

'So you're telling me to find my purpose. How can spirituality help?' Harry asked. His phone rang for a brief moment and then stopped. He checked it and said, 'Another missed call from my wife. I better check up on her . . .' He placed the phone to his ear for a minute, but there was no answer again.

'Is everything okay?' I questioned.

'She's not picking up, but I am sure everything is fine.'

I responded to his original question, 'Spirituality helps declutter your mind. This clarity gives you the ability to understand your purpose at a deeper level. You don't have to become a monk like me to practise spirituality!'

'That's what Lalita is afraid of.' Harry chuckled. 'She thinks if I get too involved, I will also shave my head and join the monastery.'

'We don't have any room for you anyway,' I joked. That really was true—we have so many people come to us to become monks that we are forced to turn some away.

'It's not just Lalita. Most people think that if you practise spirituality, your ambition to achieve is compromised. You become satisfied—Zen, like you,' he said.

'Do I look satisfied?' I asked.

'Well, sort of. I know you're busy, but don't you think you would have been more ambitious if you did not practise spirituality? I am sure some of your friends are now millionaires in America!' he said.

It was a slightly cutting remark, but I was used to it. It's one of the greatest misconceptions of spirituality. Among many others, this misconception was also addressed by Sri Krishna in the *Bhagavad Gita*.

'Let me take your mind back to the battlefield of Kurukshetra,' I said.

Does Spirituality Kill Ambition?

By now we all know what happened to Arjuna, just as he was about to engage in warfare. For us, it would not be surprising to have a nervous breakdown before battle; most of us are not trained in the military arts and would be fearful of our own deaths. But not Arjuna. He feared harming his grandfathers, his teachers and his own brothers who stood on the other side with arms in hand. He had a strong sense of compassion, but it was misplaced. Not fighting would have inundated the world with social injustice. Arjuna knew that, but knowing something and understanding it are two different things.

What is the use of a kingdom, a throne and all this opulence? I can just retire to the forest without harming anyone, he thought.

That is the exact misconception that people have about spiritualists. If you practise spirituality, then you are *satisfied* with achieving the bare minimum. Why be the managing director of a company when you can be *satisfied* being a run-of-the-mill worker? In this way, people feel that spirituality kills ambition.

Sri Krishna addressed this issue by urging Arjuna to fight. If Arjuna did not fight, the finite, neutral resources of the world would remain in the hands of the unscrupulous Kauravas, who wished to exploit them and the people under their rule. And as long as people of weak character hold all the resources, society remains in chaos. This is because the resources are used for destructive, self-aggrandizing and selfish purposes. However, if the resources are transferred to the virtuous, they are used constructively for social contribution and as a medium to serve others.

In one sense, spiritualists should be satisfied within themselves. For their personal needs, they should be happy with the bare minimum because they know that things don't bring happiness. Nevertheless, when it comes to working hard with the aim of serving others, they should not be satisfied. If they are docile and passive, things that could have been used to uplift humanity will not be. Therefore, Krishna inspired Arjuna to fight and win back the throne. In one sense, it was not the throne of the Pandavas. It was the throne of the people of their kingdom who needed the strong value-based leadership of the Pandavas for their society to thrive. Therefore, spirituality does not kill our ambition; it redirects it towards the service of others.

Most people do not have the intention of being completely selfless. To be ambitious and entrepreneurial for yourself is not wrong. There is nothing wrong with having more, earning more and living in luxury. This is coming from a monk whose life's possessions fit into a 2-metre by 3-metre room. I strongly encourage people to be successful in the world. If you have the desire to have a luxurious life, have an expensive car, have exotic holidays; there is nothing wrong with that. If by the blessings of God we have the ambition and the capacity to achieve more, we must fulfil our potential, not suppress it by force.

What is wrong is if we just live a luxurious life; the important asterisk after 'living in splendour' is to assess if we are giving back proportionately. Wealth assists selflessness by enabling one to perform charity. A person may spend crores on their wedding, but is he or she giving proportionate amounts away to help those in need? The standard of our living gives some temporary happiness to our mind, but it does not give deep satisfaction to the heart. Only giving does that. Therefore, I encourage people to passionately pursue their ambitions. But I also tell them that when God blesses us with more because of doing so, we should not only increase the standard of our living but also the standard of our giving.

'I don't have a rebuttal to that. However, let's say that my ambition does not get affected by practising spirituality, does it make me lose my cutting edge?' Harry asked vaguely.

'How so?' I replied as we neared the temple.

'There is this perception about spiritualists. If you tell someone that you practise spirituality, they look at you funny, as if your ideas and lifestyle are so backward,' he whined.

'I don't agree with that,' I said. And I didn't. 'Spiritualists are some of the most powerful people in the world. Look at civil rights activist Martin Luther King Jr, or the former President of India, Dr A.P.J. Abdul Kalam. They were people who practised spirituality.'

'That's true, but in the office—'

'So we're talking about the office!' I interrupted and laughed. 'Why did you not say so? We just talked about office politics and how an office is merely a microcosm.'

Harry blushed. 'In the office . . .' he paused. 'If you tell people that you are having a monk over for lunch, they think you are slightly odd. People feel that because you like meditation and yoga and are trying to be humble, others can take advantage of you.' I understood what Harry was trying to say.

'That is another misconception that is found in the working world: if you are trying to be virtuous, people will take advantage of you; that spiritual people will get walked over in business. Let me tell you an ancient story of why that is not true.'

The Sage and the Snake

Snakes are both respected and feared in India. According to many stereotypes, India is a land whose economy runs on income from the Taj Mahal, Goa and snake charmers! Of course, that is not true. But you cannot separate snakes and Indian culture—they are part of our landscape.

Thousands of years ago, a group of villagers approached a saintly man who was meditating inside a cave in a mountain. Years of meditation had given him the wisdom to solve any problem that came his way. Panting, the villagers approached him, and with their voices choking with fear, one of them complained, 'O revered one, please help us. There is a large venomous snake that is terrorizing the village!' The sage did not respond. He was still in deep meditation. The villagers looked at each other and then pushed the unofficial spokesman to speak again. 'You can hear the hiss of the snake for miles around. He mercilessly bites anyone on his path, regardless of whether or not he is threatened. As a consequence of this, we are all fearful to venture out in the fields by ourselves, which has led to our crops running dry. The snake's venom is not the only thing that is killing us off one by one; we are dying of starvation too! We beg of you to help us!'

The saint was naturally compassionate; most genuine, spiritual-minded people are. Understanding the gravity of the situation, he got up from his straw mat and looked at the villagers. 'Let's search for that snake,' he said. The villagers cheered, full of hope as a band of them now trailed behind the saint in search of their hissing enemy.

As they approached the dusty ghost land that was once their home, the bewitching sound of the snake echoed from the other side of the village. It approached the band of villagers with great speed, paying no regard to their pitchforks or torches of fire. The villagers fled for their lives, but the saint stood still, undeterred by the hooded creature that came to attack him. The snake's slithering and undulating green and black scales shimmered majestically in the sunlight. *What beauty!* the saint thought. Being confused since the saint was not fleeing like the rest of its prey, the snake stopped and stared at him.

'Come forth, o magnificent one,' the saint shouted out. The snake, who had never been treated with such kindness before, was mesmerized by these five words. The warmth of the saint's words replaced the warmth of the blazing fire it was used to. The snake lost all its ferocity, glided towards the saint and coiled up meekly by his feet in obeisance. The villagers, some of them hiding in the trees and some of them on the other side of the fields, couldn't hear the conversation. They looked on from a distance, astounded by what they were seeing.

'I am stunned by your beauty,' the saint said to the snake, as if they were old friends. 'But why do you haunt the villagers as you do?' The snake lowered its hood. 'Leave your destructive ways and do not terrorize the poor villagers needlessly. Stop biting them—they are no match for you. There is plenty for you to eat in the forest.' The snake bowed to the saint and resolved to leave the villagers alone. It, too, was stunned by the grace and gravity that the saint commanded.

Anyone can start a new life by making new vows. The snake had done so, too. It turned a new leaf, and scrupulously kept its promise to begin a new life of innocence, without attempting to harm anyone. From that day, the villagers became elated, their crop yield doubled, their cattle grazed without agitation and their children played games in the forest. The saint returned to his cave to continue his journey inward. A happy story? Not yet.

Several months later, the saint came down from the mountain to beg for just enough food from the villagers to keep himself alive. As he travelled to the village, he saw the same snake, coiled up near the root of a tree, lying mangled, practically dead. Its scales had fallen off; it looked emaciated and injured, with sores all over its body.

'My dear friend, what happened to you?' the saint enquired with affection.

'This is the fruit of being good,' the snake replied. Although its venom had dried up, the snake spoke with bitterness. 'I obeyed you. I gave up my tormenting ways. I left the villagers alone and stopped attacking them. But see what has happened to me. Everyone pelts me with stones, beats me with sticks, and even the children tease me and drag me mercilessly by my tail. I am now a laughing stock. However, I have kept my promise to you . . .'

The saint smiled and said, 'O snake, you have done what I have asked, but you have not fully understood my direction. I told you not to bite them, but I said nothing about stopping your ferocious hiss that could deter people for miles on end.'

The snake uncoiled itself and understood what it had to do. The villagers trembled as the hissing sound returned to the area like a bad dream. Both the villagers and the snake lived safely from then on.

'What a story!' Harry said.

'The moral is that spiritual people do not intentionally harm others, nor do they cheat others in business. However, at the same time, they do not behave timidly when it comes to work. Humility or meekness does not mean you are a pushover, it means you understand how to behave properly in all scenarios. Don't they say, *Be straightforward in two things: business and eating.* We have to understand that spirituality transforms our character; it doesn't make us fools!' I said emphatically.

Harry smiled as I continued, 'In our ambition to make money, even the sky should not be the limit. But at the same time, we should be wary of the potency money has to distract us and impel us to make compromises with our ideals. If we introspect deeply and have the regular company of spiritual-minded people, we can keep our intentions and actions clean and grow to be a massive success, based on the foundation of good character. It takes time to develop, but good character is a shining light to show us how to live our life. That's the spiritual principle of sadachar.'

Monk Mindset:

- There are many misconceptions when it comes to being a spiritual-minded person and being successful in the world.
- One is that spirituality kills our ambitions and zest to achieve. This is false because spirituality just changes our motive to achieve. It makes us want to be hugely successful so that we can have the resources to help others. The story of Krishna and Arjuna in the *Gita* explains more: Fight and achieve to help others, but be internally content in your personal life.
- Another is that spiritual people get walked over in business because of their values. The story of the sage and the snake describes how we should stick to our values but be meticulous and straightforward in business.
- Though we can make as much money as we desire, and use it to serve, we should be wary of its potential to distract us from our purpose.

SIXTEEN

Integrity and Character

Spirituality helps develop good character. It is character that shines bright when words fail to do so.

What motivates people to act righteously? Is it the lectures they listen to from charismatic speakers? Is it the entertaining philosophy they hear? Or is it the electrifying mood of the events they attend? All these can help, but according to spiritual literature, what motivates people to take action is not the conviction in their heads, but the inspiration of their hearts.

This is because people are touched more by what we do than what we say. We feel inspired by those who live with the right conduct, character and integrity, sadachar in Sanskrit. Philosophy without good character is of little or no value. There are three aspects of spirituality in practice:

- *Vichaar*: The philosophy that we seek answers from. This helps us understand how life should be lived, and how spirituality should be practised. These concepts, in turn, are the universal lighthouse principles that guide us towards living a life of value.

- *Aachaar:* Based on the philosophy is the physical action that leads to a transformation in our value system and helps us develop good conduct and character. When one's character is transformed by following even a sentence of the rich philosophy, then those actions are called aachaar.
- *Prachaar:* The good conduct of a spiritual practitioner inspires others to have faith in the philosophy and values of spirituality. Without having to give a single sermon, we can reach out to many just by being exemplary and having good character. What great men do, common men follow.

In all my talking, I had not realized but we had finally reached the temple. Harry was parked and simply listening to me patiently.

'Why did you not stop me?' I said, smiling at Harry.

'I wanted to hear more.' he replied.

'Thank you so much for driving me all the way here, and of course, for the lunch,' I said as I opened the door. I had already missed all my scheduled events for the evening, so there was no point rushing. 'Would you like to come inside?' I asked.

'That would be great,' he replied as he grabbed his keys and we both walked out into the humid air of Mumbai.

We both entered through the security gate and were greeted warmly by the guards, many of whom I have known for over fifteen years. They are part of our family. The ashram that I call home is located in Girgaum Chowpatty, Mumbai. As you walk through the entrance, you are met with a huge courtyard, with the two-storey temple carved from sandstone—the architecture is sublime! We laughed and joked as we walked towards the shoe stall—you have to take your shoes off when you enter the temple. It's a gesture that indicates cleanliness and respect for the temple and its people.

'What was the fourth wheel?' Harry said all of a sudden as he took off his shoes and handed them to the person in charge of the stall.

'Maybe we will leave that for another time,' I said, exhausted from the journey. 'I will have to come back to your house for the world-class sambar again.'

'We will feel insulted if you don't.' Harry grinned.

At that moment, Harry's phone rang. It was his wife again. 'Just a second,' he said as he stepped away from me to take the call. A few people approached me to take a picture with them, but all the while, my attention was still focused on Harry. I could hear bits of the conversation.

'Hello? How are you? Why didn't you pick up earlier?' Harry said as soon as he got connected.

'Hello?' replied a male voice on the other side.

'Who is this?' Harry said, alarmed. I noticed his face drop.

'Mr Iyer, this is Dr Shah from the Breach Candy Hospital. We were trying to get in contact with you, but a fire has taken down some of the phone towers in the area. Your wife is in the hospital. You should come . . .' The phone cut off again.

Harry dropped his phone on the floor, his face pale. I immediately ended my small talk with the guests and rushed to Harry, who was now on the balcony of the temple.

'What is it?'

'Lalita . . . Lalita is in the hospital. There is something wrong. I have to go now,' he said, panicked. He ran towards his car. I picked up his phone and ran after him.

Monk Mindset:

- Good character has the ability to change lives. It has to do with our actions, not our words.
- The principles of developing character are:
  o Vichaar: The life philosophy we follow. We must learn from it.
  o Aachaar: The action based on that philosophy. We must do it.
  o Prachaar: The good conduct that is displayed to the world through those actions. We must practise it.
- What great men do, common men follow.

WHEEL 4
SOCIAL CONTRIBUTION

SEVENTEEN

Selfless Sacrifice

You can be completely selfish, completely selfless or any of the combinations in between. Life is a journey from being selfish to becoming selfless.

Harry had run down the steps, nearly forgetting to wear his shoes. I followed him down the marble stairs and across the courtyard, clutching his phone, whose screen had cracked. The other monks looked on in confusion, as did the elderly guards. They had no idea of the news that Harry had just received. His wife was in hospital, and the doctor had called him to come. Can you imagine the thoughts that must have been going through his head? The pain caused by the thought of losing a loved one can often be just as hurtful as actually losing them.

Harry unlocked the car from a distance. He flung open the door, ignoring the man standing close by, selling fresh coconut water from his cart.

'You don't have to come, please. Thank you so much for all your time. I am sure you must have so much to do,' Harry said across the car bonnet to me. It was more important to be there with Harry than to attend to what I had planned. Painful situations are easier to deal with when you have friends by your side to support you. Although I am a monk and have a lot of official duties, I like to be a friend to people I care about. That is a deeper, more personal connection.

'I am sorry but I am coming with you, whether you like it or not,' I said, opening the passenger door. We both sat down, seat belts clicked, and he reversed out on to the road, not seeing if any other cars were coming. We had to get to the hospital fast.

Although I had been sitting in the same seat for over three hours, the whole car seemed completely different. In fact, the Mumbai that I was used to looked different. The mood in the car was tense, which also affected how I was perceiving the world. Our whole world view can change in just an instant, when we hear such life-changing news. How do we behave in those situations? How do *friends* behave in those situations when someone has found out something so upsetting?

It was either sweat or tears, or a mixture of both, that was running down Harry's face as he scanned his mind for side roads to dodge the traffic that we were carelessly commuting through just minutes ago. As he tapped on the steering wheel, pressed his horn and repeatedly checked his phone for any sign of news, he blurted out, 'What was wheel four?'

I thought he was trying to be polite and carry on with our previous conversation.

'Wheel four?' I said. I was totally surprised. I was not even thinking about the wheels of the car at that moment. It was not a time for speaking about the essence of life—this was a moment of emergency. It was a time for him to drive fast and act, and for me to support him with my friendship. In times of great calamity, sometimes the right thing to do is to just be there. I wished I had some herbal tea. But I spoke. 'Wheel four has to do with being selfless, and making a social contribution. But let's talk about that another time. Let's focus on reaching your wife—who I am sure is doing perfectly fine.' He nodded in agreement and focused on the road. We were already zooming past Kemps Corner, ignoring any signals that were telling us to stop and obey the laws of the road. All we needed was a siren on top of our car.

Thoughts travel faster than words and they are not always in the right order. In the same vein, I will present this wheel on selflessness quickly here. In a matter of ten minutes from Kemps Corner to the hospital, as we travelled at lightning speed, I thought of all these things. My training as a monk implies that the practice of selflessness is meant to be somewhat natural to me, but like most of us, I still have a long way to go.

As Harry drove, I rested my hand on his shoulder in silent consolation and thought of how he at that moment was representing wheel four: to be selfless and to give back.

The Ice Cream, the Candle and the Oxygen Mask

Sanskrit is one of the oldest languages in the world. It is the philosophical language of Hinduism and other faiths originating from it. Considered to be the language of the gods, it sounds elegant and sophisticated and the script is called *deva-nagri*—from the city of the gods. If you want to call someone a donkey in Sanskrit, one of the words for it is *vaishakanandan*. How charming that sounds! The word for ice cream is interesting, too. It is *dughda-sharkara-yukta-hima-ghana-gola-gattu*. Or if you want to add a little flavour, mango ice cream is *amra-dughda-sharkara-yukta-hima-ghana-gola-gattu*. It takes practice to be able to speak Sanskrit for sure. I am a true fan of Sanskrit, but a bigger fan of ice cream. There is no dessert as delicious as ice cream, especially in the tropics. However, the ideology behind the ice cream is: enjoy your life before it melts. It symbolizes hedonism; to savour every moment of your life through personal enjoyment.

On the other hand, the candle is symbolic of another ideology: to give light to others before it melts. Both ice creams and candles melt, but their reasons for doing so are completely different. The candle is formed from wax. Its very essence is burnt just to give light for other people to see. This is the selfless nature of a candle.

On the spectrum below where do you lie?

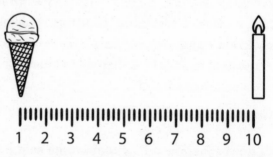

I am sure that you do not think of yourself as completely selfish. Nor can you put yourself down as completely selfless. We are all somewhere in between. Just because we cannot be candles fully, it does not mean we should simply remain selfish at the ice-cream end. The journey of life is moving from being an ice cream to being a candle. That is the purpose of everyone's life at the core: to share, give and contribute to others.

'But why have we discussed three wheels about ourselves first, then?' you might ask. 'If the purpose of life is to give to others, why have we discussed understanding ourselves, being happy at work and in our relationships? Does this not sound selfish?'

To understand this we have to learn from the oxygen mask.

A lot of stories in this book have been from my travels. Every flight has safety instructions that we all must follow. Some are about routine things like wearing a seat belt while others are for emergencies, which we hope that we never have to use, like wearing a life jacket or an oxygen mask.

As the members of the cabin crew demonstrate the oxygen mask on the plane, the cabin supervisor makes an announcement, 'If there is a lack of oxygen supply in the cabin, oxygen masks will drop down from the panel above your heads. To activate the flow of oxygen, pull the mask towards you sharply, place it firmly over your nose and mouth, secure the elastic band behind your head and breathe normally. *Make sure that your mask is securely fastened before you help children, infants or others.*' Does this last part not sound selfish? Surely we should be helping others before we help ourselves! However, it should be understood that unless we help ourselves and breathe in oxygen, we cannot be of any real help to others. We can only share wealth with others if we possess wealth. Similarly, we can love others only if we know what it feels like to be loved. We can only bring hope to others if we feel hope for ourselves. In conclusion, we can only give to others what we possess.

If we try to help others without being satisfied and balanced in the first three wheels, we will not be able to give them something of value, and we could even experience 'compassion fatigue'. Compassion fatigue is a state of stress experienced by those who help others to the extent that they start suffering because of their preoccupation with the suffering of others. It can be detrimental to care too much; caregivers who do not focus on self-care can develop destructive behaviours over time. Therefore, we need to be slightly selfish to start our journey on a sure footing in order to reach the stage where we can afford to be completely selfless without causing damage to our own well-being.

I do believe it is possible to be completely selfless, but it is a journey, a process, and not a single event. It takes wisdom to know when we are being selfless and when we are simply causing harm to ourselves by being 'overcaring'. The principle and practice of service involves being somewhere in the middle on the ice cream to candle spectrum: to be selfish yet selfless.

My hand was still on Harry's shoulder. We had become even closer in the last few hours. Remember, revealing the mind and allowing another person to reveal their mind to you breeds deep friendship. At that moment, Harry was displaying complete selflessness. His only thought was helping his wife. In the process, he had nearly forgotten his phone and shoes at the temple. The rage he had spoken with about his wife earlier seemed completely pacified. Sometimes it is in testing situations that we realize how much love we feel for someone.

As we zoomed in and out of traffic, back along the shore, I turned to Harry and said, 'Don't worry, Harry. Everything is going to be fine. See how much love you have for your wife.' He gave me half a smile in gratitude, and then focused his attention fully on the road again. I returned to my thoughts.

Monk Mindset:

- The philosophy of an ice cream is: Enjoy it before it melts.
- The philosophy of a candle is: Give light to others before it melts.
- In order to be happy, we should shift our attitude from being an ice cream to a candle, from being selfish to selfless. This is shown through service.
- We must be wary of compassion fatigue. This means we must have all our wheels balanced as we try to help others. This is the principle of being selfishly selfless.

EIGHTEEN

Family First

The first step in selflessness is to practise it with our family.

Our journey of selflessness from an ice cream to a candle must start somewhere. Often, people can display selflessness outside their home. People may help out in their community, or at temples or schools, and some may even make sure that they get a selfie to announce to the world that they have helped. But at home, they may not express the same service mentality. I believe that selflessness starts at home; with the ones we love the most. Are we doing what we can to help them? Are we there for them to help them physically as well as emotionally? Relationships at home can work well only if all parties have low expectations of each other, but high expectations of themselves to help the other.

At this moment, Harry was an example of serving the one you love. Another thought that came to my mind was of Lata Khare, whose story of sacrifice for her husband deeply touched my heart.

Running Marathons

Lata Bhagavan Khare was a sixty-five-year-old resident of a small village. Her life was simple. She and her husband would go daily to a landowner's farm and make just enough to survive; their house was small, but the food they got from the farm filled their stomachs.

The small amount of money they had saved throughout their lives was spent on getting their three daughters married. Now that their responsibilities were complete, they enjoyed the simple pleasures of life and each other's company. They were inseparable and understood each other completely. Their relationship was a testament to the principle that you did not need luxury to be happy.

One day after coming back from the farm, her husband told her that he did not feel so well. She tried all sorts of herbal medicines to help him, but he would not get better. The local government hospital diagnosed him with a serious infection, and they recommended that she go to a bigger hospital that had more facilities to do further tests. Lata was bewildered. They hardly had enough money for the fare to get a ride to the hospital, let alone the expensive tests prescribed by the doctors. With tears in her eyes, she told her husband the news and felt overwhelmed with helplessness. How could she let her husband die in her arms?

Plucking up her courage and leaving her ego at the door, she then begged from her neighbours and relatives to gather money to go to the bigger hospital to save her husband's life. With the help she had received, they got to the big hospital. This was not the sort of place that they were used to being in, so they felt very uncomfortable and out of place. Some people at the hospital gave them strange looks; others ignored them as if they were invisible. Undeterred, Lata mustered more courage and asked to see a doctor. The people at the reception took an initial fee, nearly everything they had, and asked them to wait outside a doctor's room until they were called. She sat there, as the important-looking people roamed the hallways speaking terms she didn't understand. Her middle name, Bhagavan, means 'God' in Sanskrit, and that is whom she prayed to, hoping that he would save her husband and dearest friend.

When the time came, her husband was called in. After an examination, the doctor handed her a list of further tests and prescribed medications and a recommendation to stay at the hospital. Lata sank back into her chair as her world suddenly turned dark. *I have no money, I have nowhere to go, how will I afford this to help the love of my life?* she thought. With tears flowing down her cheeks, she and her husband solemnly walked out of the hospital.

They could not afford the commercial prices of the hospital canteen, so they stopped by a samosa–wallah at the bus stop. They bought two for the bus journey back to their village. All Lata could think about was that this could be her husband's last meal. The samosa–wallah wrapped their snack up in a newspaper and handed it to her with a smile. As she ate her samosa and chutney from the newspaper pack, she saw the headline: 'Baramati Marathon: Prize Money Available'. Her heart skipped a beat, but regained its rhythm fast. She would need it pumping for the race she was about to run.

The next day as everyone lined up at the start of the race, in their running gear, Lata Khare stood there in her red-checked Maharashtrian-style sari. Barefoot, and with tears in her eyes, she argued with the organizers to allow her to run in the marathon, but they refused. She was sixty-five! In trying to save her husband, they did not want her to pass away. After an hour of begging and pleading, they finally agreed to let her run and pinned a number on her clothes. As she began running, people turned to look at her and laughed. Many of them had thought that she must have come with her daughter or son to watch them participate in the race; they were shocked to see her running. She took no notice of the other sniggering competitors.

It was a sight for sore eyes. Teenagers and young adults who had been practising for months for this race lined up next to an old lady who had hitched her sari above her ankles. She had never run a race in her life, to say nothing of a marathon. Little did her competitors know that they were about to get schooled by someone who was old enough to be their grandmother. She could not think of anything else but the love she had for her husband. This race was a matter of life and death. What were a few pebbles and rocks to stop her progress?

Lata ran like the wind with one focus—the finish line. Her feet began to bleed, her sari became soaked with sweat, but she kept running. It would have been an achievement even if she could just finish the race. The people who witnessed this spectacle cheered her on; they were touched by her reason for running.

It would be a pointless story if she did not win. There was no award for participation but she had done it! The organizers of the race could not believe that Lata Khare, a sixty-five-year-old Maharashtrian woman from a small village, had won the race. The crowds on the streets of Baramati clapped for her and celebrated her victory. She was a local hero, but she did not care for the attention.

She collected her winnings, marched into the hospital and got her husband the best treatment. At the same time, she got a few bandages for her feet! Her only motive was to save her husband. As they say, the most powerful force in the world is love. Lata went on to win for the next two years consecutively, but that's another story.

I wanted to tell Harry this story, but it was not the right time. His situation was very similar to Lata's. Just as she ran to help her love, Harry was doing everything he could at that moment to help his. Selflessness starts with our family, but it should not just end there. To expand our circle of selflessness, we should help those outside of our immediate care and affection too.

Monk Mindset:

- On one level, we practise selflessness in helping our family. Our day-to-day sacrifices to maintain our family relations are acts of selflessness. We do not necessarily have to run marathons like Lata Khare to display our devotion to those we love.
- Our circle of selflessness should not end with our family. We should help those outside of our immediate care and affection too.

NINETEEN

The Nation Narrative

*We can increase our scope of selflessness beyond our family by
serving our community, city or even nation.*

We zigzagged in the traffic, using all our knowledge of the
city to get to the hospital via back roads. It is incredible how
much you miss when you just stick to the beaten path. I
was seeing parts of the city that I had not seen before, and
people were shocked to see a high-end car with a monk in the
passenger seat zoom through their neighbourhood. The roar
of the engine was deafening to the city-folk dwelling in these
parts who were carrying out their daily duties of congregating
and drinking chai. To us, however, the roar meant that we
would get to Lalita sooner.

It could have been because we were in deep conversation on
the way to the temple that we missed it, but going a different
route we saw the cause of the traffic. Mumbai had ground to
a halt because of the flames that were engulfing a building.
Billowing smoke formed spirals in the sky as it rose from the
top of the three-storey apartment. It was a terrifying sight.
Traffic built up around the scene as people stopped and stared,

and the police tried their best to divert both. The red lights of fire engines lined the streets, and we even saw some soldiers from the armed forces there to assist them.

My attention fell upon two men—one a firefighter and another a soldier—who were working hand in hand to grab one of the long hoses from the fire engines. They both ran with it together and stood right next to the blaze trying to defeat it. In times of calamity, teamwork makes all the difference; people must come together. The sacrifice these men were making reminded me of another man, from the Indian Army—my friend, Brigadier Sunil Kumar N.V. When he was telling me his story, he choked up. And since it wasn't common for a man from the army to get emotional, I had asked him, 'What's wrong?' Though he said nothing, I guessed he was simply expressing the love he felt for his men as they bravely served their country. I marvelled at how widening your circle of influence to help your community and nation is more fulfilling than just helping your family. Sunil Kumar's stories offer the perfect examples of how this works.

Serving the Country

'The leaves crunched as our Indian commando team walked in a single file surrounded by the overgrowth of the Sri Lankan jungle,' Sunil Kumar began. 'Each of our commandos had black-and-green warpaint on their faces to complete the camouflage. Their fingers lurked around their semi-automatic rifles. They could not trust the rustling and singing of the tropical birds in the canopy. An uneasy silence fell over the troop as they looked at each other, knowing what was coming.

'All of a sudden, birds flew from the top of a tree as they heard the gunshots. It was the Liberation Tigers of Tamil Eelam attacking our Indian Peacekeeping Force. AK-47 bullets from the Tamil Tigers clawed into our ambushed task force. We lay flat on the ground in defence and, following the echoes of the storm of bullets, fired eastwards.

'Most of our men escaped. We weren't sure how many were left,' Sunil continued. 'It was 1988, and technology was not as advanced as it is today. It would take some time to find out how many casualties there were across the jungle floor. We got a crackling call to our unit that one of our commandos was critically injured and had to be evacuated. Where was he exactly? We didn't know. How badly was he injured? We didn't know. How many men were around him? You see the picture of uncertainty developing. However, we were called in to help and rescue him.

'We started our treacherous trek towards him. On our journey, we saw the footprints of the men who had gone through the jungle before us. The long, winding path followed a freshwater stream, taking us through unfamiliar territory. We reached the site quicker than we'd expected. I suppose when you know someone is in danger, you work harder to help them. We could still hear gunshots in the distance, but we reached our man relatively unharmed,' Kumar added.

'Even before seeing the soldier, you could smell the wretched stench of blood and flesh. He was so badly injured that some of his internal organs had fallen out through the deep cuts in his body. Blood gushed from him and he cried in pain. "I don't want to die," he screamed when he saw us.

"Tell my wife and children I love them. Tell my countrymen I love them," he continued, unable to hold back his emotions. It was an urgent situation and we had to get him out of there at any cost. Any more noise would attract the Tamil Tigers to pounce on us.

'We opened the stretcher we were carrying and quickly shifted him onto that. First aid was tough in a situation where adrenaline was flowing like oxygen. "We have a casualty. Calling for helicopter evac.!" I spoke into my portable radio.

'"No can do," it replied. "The jungle is too hot and there is not a field in sight." They could not risk having the helicopter blown out of the air. We had to find another way out of that hell and take our man to a military hospital.

'Considering his condition, we only had one choice,' the brigadier said. 'We picked him up on the stretcher and moved quickly to the nearest road, where we flagged down a car and took control. I am a Keralite and, hence, I managed to pass off as Sri Lankan. It was easy for us to convince the driver to take us to the hospital as we blended in with the locals. It was a dangerous move. If the person whose car we were in was a sympathizer of the Tamil Tigers, we would have no hope. They were notorious for randomly stopping vehicles. But finally, we raced through the jungle and managed to get to a military hospital just in time for our injured comrade to live to tell the tale.

'After a few months he was back in the unit, ready to go out on duty again. This was the camaraderie within the army; we were willing to sacrifice for each other and the nation. It is this spirit that motivates us to serve more.'

Sunil Kumar did not just talk about the heat of the jungle. He also mentioned his time on the highest battlefield on earth—the Siachen Glacier in the Himalayas. Talking about the team spirit in the army, he said: 'I was commanding a group of men to protect the frozen Indian border, which lay on a huge chunk of ice. Life is unpredictable on the glacier. There can be avalanches, which can bury you under tonnes of falling snow. Or, in my opinion, something worse: the glacier is known for its random crevices, ice cracking open, creating canyons 100–200 feet deep. While walking without being alert, if you fall through, which *has* happened in the past, your rescue would be hopeless. Your body would freeze as temperatures plummet to -100 degrees Celsius inside the abyss.

'We came up with a way to stay safe together. We tied ourselves with a long rope, so if one person fell in the crevice, the others could crack ice picks into the ground and then we could all pull him back up. We were risking our lives, not just from fighting in the war, but from the deadly cold that directly risks the heart and the body. It was our team spirit that allowed us to put our lives on the line for each other and the country,' Brigadier Kumar recounted.

My mind was frozen on the Siachen Glacier as the tyres screeched. I was thinking about how all of us could sleep peacefully at night only because the tough men and women of the Indian Armed Forces stand ready to face any challenges, even ready to sacrifice their lives, to protect the nation and its citizens. The least we can do to pay back our military is, as a nation and as citizens, to try to be worthy of the sacrifices they make for us.

We had arrived at the hospital. I diverted my full attention back to Harry as he slouched in his seat, holding the bottom of the steering wheel. He paused and breathed, changing his mood from the manic nature of his driving. 'What if she doesn't make it?' he said, looking me in the eye.

'Make what?' I replied.

'What if she is taken away from me?' he cried. *It's in moments of great grief that we understand what people mean to us*, I thought.

I said nothing as I leaned across the seat to give him a hug. He wiped his eyes with the handkerchief in his blazer pocket. It had been an emotionally tiring day for him, and it was about to get even more so. He exhaled and opened his door. I leapt out of the passenger side and followed him as he entered the hospital to meet his fate.

Monk Mindset:

- When we expand the circle of selflessness, we can effectively serve our community and nation. This is shown by the heroic efforts of the soldiers who keep us safe, and the civil servants who help run our nations.

TWENTY

Service Brings Joy

In Sanskrit, service is called seva. *Adding a spiritual element to our* seva *can make it more fulfilling.*

The hospital was noisy. Doctors in white coats walked around with a sense of confidence, and rightly so. Their actions could mean the difference between life and death, between grieving or happy homes, between dreams achieved or buried for good. They had the power to make a difference. Harry rushed to the reception. 'How can I help?' The receptionist smiled at Harry, immune to the urgency in his manner. She did a double take when she saw me, interested in my unusual apparel.

'We need the room number for Lalita—Harry said, but was interrupted by the receptionist answering the phone.

'Just a moment, sir . . . Hospital, how can I help you?' The receptionist had tuned out to answer her phone. Harry groaned, clenched his teeth, tapped his fingers on the counter and gave the receptionist a deadly stare. He spoke louder. 'I need the room number for Lalita . . .' The receptionist took no notice of Harry's demeanour. She swivelled her chair slightly and twirled the winding cord of the phone around her finger.

'Iyer. Heart rate is stable, pyrexia, emesis since arrival,' a young doctor said to an older one, as he followed him. The older doctor looked important and commanded the respect of ten, who seemed like students following him. They were captivated by every word he spoke. Harry overheard his surname and barged into the intimate circle of medical students with their tutor.

'Did you say Iyer?' Harry asked the student. The student looked at his tutor, unsure of how to reply.

'We cannot reveal any confidential patient information to you, sir,' the student said cautiously.

'I am Harry Iyer, husband of Lalita Iyer. When you said Iyer, did you mean her? Lalita Iyer? Where is she?' Harry said, ignoring the student and directing his question at their senior.

'Mr Iyer?' the tutor said. 'Hello, my name is Dr Harshil Shah, we spoke on the phone earlier.' Harry shook the doctor's hand with both of his.

'Where is Lalita? What is going on?' he said, still holding the doctor's hand, knowing well that Dr Shah was his lifeline to his wife.

'Please follow me, sir. We are just running some tests,' Dr Shah replied. He had not taken much notice of me yet. He sped away up some stairs, getting handed medical charts by nurses wearing white nursing caps along the way. Harry chased the doctor. The medical students chased Harry, excited as if they were now seeing something of value, and I chased the whole group, knowing that I had to be there for my friend.

Harry and I were both stationed in the first-floor waiting area by the doctor, who said we might have to wait for some time before we could see Lalita. He confirmed that she was on this floor and then disappeared just as fast with his band of trainees. We did not have much idea of what was going on. Harry closed his eyes and put his hands together. It looked as though he was praying, but I was not sure. His face was solemn. One after another, the doctors were calling in people for either an appointment or to see their loved ones. It was only after thirty minutes had passed that Dr Shah called for Harry. 'Harry Iyer, Lalita is now well enough to see you.'

'What was the problem?' Harry said while walking over to him. 'Will she be okay? Where is she?' He went down the corridor into a room where his wife was.

As I sat in the waiting area, fearing the worst, I looked around, watching the doctors interacting with their patients—with love and compassion—and I thought about the instinct that drives a spiritualist to act. It is one of seva or selfless service. My mind went back in time to the start of February, to the hospital that our community runs on Mira Road, Mumbai, and the values that the doctors working there have been inspired by. Many of them were stationed in the sacred land of Barsana, giving their time, skills and hearts to serve those who needed it the most in their annual free Dental and Eye Camp. I remembered the stories one of my friends from London, Vinay Raniga, a dental student himself at the time, told me about the camp.

Devotion at the Dental Camp

The land of Barsana, two hours' drive south of New Delhi, is sacred to those who practise bhakti yoga. It is home to people who have been brought up to make spirituality their life's focus, to imbibe the qualities of selflessness and loving service. However, these very people do not have the best healthcare systems. Many of them need glasses as they cannot see, or need dental treatment as they cannot eat.

The Barsana Dental and Eye Camp provides relief for thousands of villagers in the area at least once a year, and Vinay had come to help out at the dental camp.

The dental camp turns an ashram building a few minutes' walk from the famous Sriji temple into a pop-up dental clinic for the week. Weeks before the camp, a few of the volunteers go around to the neighbouring villages, advertising the opportunity the villagers have to improve their health. The camp begins at eight in the morning, but by 4 a.m., there is already a queue of hundreds waiting for their chance to get their problems addressed.

As the camp starts, a few dentists do a brief assessment of patients, giving them a signed sheet of the treatment they need. Patients are sent to departments accordingly. Some need fillings, others need teeth extracted and a few need a full set of upper and lower dentures.

Vinay told me, 'I was helping in the area that deals with making these dentures for elderly patients. After begging and convincing my professors in London, I had been given permission to take some time out from my course to attend the camp. Up until this point, I had never even made a denture, let alone the forty we were about to make in a week. I remember thinking that I wanted to match these colleagues, not just in the skill they had in dentistry, but the love they displayed to these materially poverty-stricken people who could give them nothing but their heartfelt blessings.

'I was guided by the qualified dentists on all the procedures, and was slightly embarrassed that I did not know the basic terms they were explaining. After a few practice sessions, I decided that I wanted to complete a set of dentures myself for a patient, working on all the stages from start to finish. That was when I met Nangu,' Vinay continued.

'Nangu was a seventy-two-year-old woman born and brought up in Barsana. She had never left the village, and lived a simple life tending to her cows and farm. Whenever she came to me she wore a modest purple sari, using a part of it to cover her head, and a tattered orange sweater. She lived in poverty, in a simple thatched house, which had few possessions, but it was obvious that she possessed a deeper wealth within her in the form of love for her goddess Srimati Radharani.

'"I am a dental student from London," I said to her in my broken Hindi. "I am here to make you a set of dentures. Would you like that?"

'She nodded and spoke about her problems in having to eat without any teeth. You could see the appreciation in her eyes and what having teeth would mean to her. She was radiant and showered me with her grandmotherly love. Because we had lab technicians on site, a process that would normally take months was shortened to just three days. On the third day, it was time to hand the dentures over to Nangu.

'As she walked back into the room, you could feel the anticipation within her. It was like a child excited to open their presents at Christmas or Diwali. I tried the upper denture in her mouth first and then the lower. I was heartbroken at what I saw. Her lower teeth were in front of her upper teeth. "What shall I do?" I pestered one of the other senior dentists who was more experienced than I.

'She is posturing forward. You need to let her get used to it,' he said calmly while treating his own patient. After years of not having teeth, Nangu had got used to pushing her lower jaw forward to eat, but that could be corrected by helping her practise putting it in the right place.

Thank God! I thought. Although this was volunteering and service, and there was no monetary pressure involved, I still felt great commitment to make sure Nangu got a good set of teeth. All I could think was, this woman is like my very own grandmother!

'After some time, her lower jaw fell into place and the dentures came together,' Vinay said. 'I held her hand to help her get up from the garden chair she was sitting on. Again, this was a makeshift dental clinic! I slowly helped her get to a mirror that was hanging in the open courtyard next to the room. I told her to close her eyes as we walked. As she stood in front of the mirror, I told her to open them. For the first time in fifteen years she was seeing shiny new teeth. She tapped her teeth together, cautiously trying to get used to her bite. Tears were streaming down her face as she moved closer to the mirror, wiping away some of the dust that covered it. I could not help but cry too. She sat on the stairs next to the mirror and I squatted down next to her. She stroked my hair with affection and I folded my hands to receive her blessings. "What does this mean to you?" I asked her. "It means that I can eat and chew properly. It means that my stomach can be filled at night," she said as she smiled and her eyes glistened. It was a heart-touching moment for me, to know that my service had added some value to her life.'

Seva

So what is driving Vinay to serve? What is driving all the people who apply spirituality in their life to help others? When we connect to ourselves and with the divine, our understanding, values and paradigms transform. When we practise spirituality sincerely, we obtain a higher perspective on life. We understand that living for ourselves has the potential to satisfy the mind and senses, but not the deep core of our hearts.

When we live superficial lives, dedicated to serving ourselves, we are like surfers: riding the waves, but not seeing what is beneath them. We may satisfy our own needs and concerns by doing so, but we will never be truly fulfilled. However, when we practise spirituality, we become like divers: we submerge ourselves underneath the turbulent waves to find a pleasure much deeper, beyond hedonistic ideals. That profound joy is only possible when one feels love to serve others. And how is that love maintained? Through being connected to God through spirituality. Love for God is composed of three things:

- *Right Action*: We must express our love through the correct action. We must behave and act in a way that is in line with spiritual principles.
- *Right Intention*: Our intentions must be selfless. When we want something for ourselves in return for our service, such as prestige or money, our intentions become tainted. Just as distilling water multiple times makes it cleaner, continuously checking our intentions makes them purer.

- *Right Mood*: We must serve in a way that is favourable for our growth. Serving because 'we have to' or because 'it's the right thing to do' is good, but it's not the same as serving from the depths of our hearts.

When that love is within our hearts, it erupts and naturally wants to be given to others. I once heard a saint cite the example of a bumblebee.

'Once a bumblebee was flying and saw an open jar of honey. Out of excitement, it decided to dive into the jar, completely covering itself with the delicious, sticky liquid. As it flew out of the jar, it rushed to tell all the other bumblebees what had happened, and in the process, a few drops of honey started flying out of its mouth at all the other bees. For all its friends, this was incredible. They were getting honey just because of the enthusiasm and actions of that one bee. Similarly, when we have deep love for God, it becomes natural for us to want to share that with everyone. That is because a person connected to God has a compassionate and empathetic heart. The true symptom of someone who is experiencing genuine love for God is that they experience compassion and the pain of the suffering that people go through in this world,' the saint said.

Likewise, Jesus Christ said in the Bible, 'The highest commandment is to love thy God with all thy soul and all thy might and all thy heart.' He then said that because of following the highest commandment of loving God we begin to 'love thy neighbour as thy self'. This means when we become spiritually minded and experience the love of God, we feel compassion for the pain of others. In Sanskrit it is called *para dukha dukhi*, one who feels pain in the pain of others. In the modern world, people sometimes become *para dukha sukhi*, where they take pleasure in seeing the pain of others. However, true compassion stems from spirituality.

I could understand the pain that Harry was feeling, but I was not at the level of *para dukha dukhi*, one who truly feels the pain others are going through. Still, I endeavoured to comfort him and give him words of solace all through this stressful time. Several tense minutes passed as I sat in the waiting area. I was thinking about the worst that could happen and prayed that my mind's conjecture be incorrect.

'Mr Das? Mr Gaur Gopal Das?' Dr Shah said. 'Harry and Lalita would like to see you in their room.' I gulped, and wrapped my brown cotton shawl around myself, either to protect me from the heavy air-conditioning or subconsciously from the news I was about to hear. I walked down the gloomy corridor to room 116, knocked on the door and turned its handle slowly.

Lalita was lying down on the bed and Harry was by her side, holding her hand while sitting on a small stool. The nurse in the room excused herself so that they could share their news. I stood awkwardly in front of them.

'We have some news to share with you,' Harry said. I was glad I was in a hospital, because my heart was pumping blood around my body faster than I could think. 'But it's not what you think.'

He let Lalita take over. 'Harry and I have been trying for a child for a long time, and today I got the news that the intense morning-sickness I was suffering from is actually a good sign. Harry and I are expecting a child!'

I breathed a huge sigh of relief and joined Harry, his mother and Lalita, congratulating them profusely, as they smiled and laughed uncontrollably.

The hospital, which had seemed dark and dreary just moments ago—a place of death and disease—was now transformed into a place that was offering new life.

The flavour of the joy I tasted in the hospital room that day was out of this world.

Monk Mindset:

- In Sanskrit, service is called seva. Adding a spiritual element to our seva can make it more fulfilling. Based on our connection to God, we utilize our skills and potential to serve others. We learnt about Vinay at the Barsana Dental Camp.
- From spiritual practice comes seva: 'The true symptom of someone who is experiencing genuine love for God is that they experience compassion and pain for the suffering that people go through in this world.'
- We have to do the right action, with the right intention and in the right mood, for it to be classed as spiritual.

APPENDIX I

Forgiveness Worksheet

1. Identify the cause

Think of a person you want to forgive, and what you want to forgive them for.

Now sit back and relax. Breathe in, hold your breath for a few seconds, and breathe out. This exercise may release a lot of emotion—let it all come naturally.

Write it down in the space below.

For example
'I want to forgive Sam for raising his voice at me in front of all our friends.'

....
....

....
....

....
....

2. Look at the situation from the other person's perspective

Put yourself in the other person's shoes. Try to think about the situation and understand why they may have treated you in this way. It is important to understand the intention of the person and why they may have acted in the way they did towards you. When we understand the reason why the person may have acted in that way, it may make it easier for us to forgive.

Example:

'Sam seemed stressed that day. I think he may have been having some family issues. That could be the reason he spoke to me in an unusual manner.'

....

....

....

....

....

....

....

....

3. Confirm the other person's thoughts

To confirm what the person's thoughts were when they acted towards you in a certain way, you may do one of the following things.

a) Approach the person directly. Use tact to understand their thought process. A normal conversation may help reveal why they acted the way they did. Note: You do not want to go into this meeting with an accusatory attitude, as it may backfire if things get emotional.

b) Talk to someone who can help you understand that person's current situation; this could be a family member or close friend of that person.

c) If A and B are not possible, then wait until more unfolds. Let time reveal more.

Write it down in the space below.

....
....

....
....

....
....

....
....

4. Foresee difficulties that may arise, but also try to see the benefits of forgiving this person

When trying to forgive someone, there may be situations and emotions that may replay in your mind and make it difficult to completely let go.

You may be feeling hurt, anger, injustice: whatever it is, write it down below.

Counteract the feelings of hurt with the benefits of letting that feeling go.

Example:

'I think forgiving Sam will be hard because I know I did nothing wrong in this situation. Overlooking the fact that I was right and forgiving him will be difficult for me. However, it will help our relationship grow, so it is the right thing to do.'

....

....

....

....

....

....

....

....

5. Remember all the good things that person has done for you

Recalling all the good things the person has done for you will help you on your journey in forgiving them.

For example:

'I want to forgive Sam because it will mean that when I speak to him, I will no longer feel uneasy and replay the incident in my mind. I am so grateful for everything that Sam has done for me over the years.'

....

....

....

....

....

....

....

....

6. Think of how you want to live after forgiving

- Forgive and forget. (Therefore trust the person again.)
- Forgive, monitor and then trust. (Look to see if the person has improved their behaviour before trusting them again.)
- Forgive and not trust. (You can forgive the person but decide to no longer have a trusting relationship with them.)
- Forgive and take action. (You may forgive the person and need to take action, either legal or practical. Example: you may forgive your spouse for cheating on you, but you may still decide to live separate lives.)

In the space below, write how you want to live after forgiving the person and why you want to live in this way.

Example:

'I am going to forgive and forget about how James spoke to me the other day, because this was a rare occurrence in which James was not his usual, polite self.'

....
....
....
....
....
....

7. Look at your Forgiveness affirmation.

You should have noted:

- The person you want to forgive, and what you want to forgive them for.
- The situation from the other person's perspective (in your opinion).
- Confirm the other person's intention towards you.
- Any difficulties that may arise in trying to forgive the person.
- All the good things that the person has done for you.
- Whether you want to forgive and forget; forgive and not trust; forgive, monitor and then trust; or forgive and take action.

Ikigai Worksheet

Identifying Purpose

1. Write down a job/skill that you love doing and that you are good at.

What you love: When you love doing something, it may give you excitement even if you're not getting paid to do it. Reflect on the times in your life when you've felt like this. Do these memories have a common thread running through them?

What you're good at: To understand if you are good at something, get honest feedback from the people around you. For example, if you think you are good at public speaking, do the people around you feel that you are good at speaking? Are the people giving you advice experts in their field to be giving you such advice?

....
....
....
....

2. Can you make a living from your passions?

Some people do not want to get paid for doing what they love. That is okay! However, many are working dead-end jobs while they dream about a life in which they are fully dedicated to their purpose. But full dedication also takes into account the practicalities of life! Many of you may have children whose tuition fees need to be paid; or mortgages that wait for no one. Please use the space below to briefly state how you could get paid to do what you love.

....

....

....

....

....

....

3. Can you turn your passions into purpose?

The happiest people are those helping others. Does this passion help you contribute to the world? Your passion is for you, but once you figure out how to use it to serve others, it becomes your purpose.

You can turn your passion into your purpose by using one of the three R's:

Relevance: Is your passion directly relevant to helping others? For example, being a teacher can be a rewarding profession: you can earn a living, while simultaneously enriching young minds.

Resources: Does your situation allow you to use its benefits to help others? This could be your status to influence change, your money to help with philanthropy or your network to change hearts.

Remainder of your time: Your situation may give you flexibility, to have the time to carry out what you're passionate about outside of your day-to-day work. There are many people who work all day at the office, but come alive serving the homeless afterwards.

I should stress that purpose does not mean a grand statement to 'change the world'. It could mean having grand intentions to change the world in a small way. That small contribution may feed into a larger network of people working together to help. For example, if you want to help the homeless, can you connect with an organization or group that resonates with you?

Using the space below, please identify how you are willing to use your passion to serve others.

....

....

....

....

....

....

....

....

Common struggles that hold you back from finding your ikigai:

- My current job pays well, I cannot give it up.
- I do not know where to begin.
- I don't know if I am good enough to get paid at what I love.
- I do not have the support of my family.

These are common reasons why people fail to find their ikigai.

Write down what you feel your struggles may be, and identify ways to overcome these.

....
....

....
....

....
....

....
....

Initially, you may not be able to do the job you love full-time. However, you can start by working on it in your spare time.

Confirming Your Ikigai

Now that you have found your ikigai, confirm it with someone who is your friend, who is an expert in that field and who has your best interests at heart. Not everyone is friends with an 'expert', you may argue. But be wary of asking people who have no understanding of the subjects that interest you. A doctor cannot tell you what is wrong with your car, and a mechanic cannot tell you why you have a cough.

In the space below, note what the people you have asked have said about your ikigai findings.

....

....

....

....

....

....

....

....

Acknowledgements

I offer my sincerest gratitude to His Divine Grace A.C. Bhaktivedanta Swami Srila Prabhupada, whose teachings have been the foundation of how I live my life. My own spiritual master, Radhanath Swami, who has been my inspiration and example in living a life of integrity and good character, imparted these teachings to me. He not only encouraged me to write this book but also facilitated my stay at the peaceful Govardhan Ecovillage so that I could complete it without any distractions. My limitless thanks to him!

Thank you to Gauranga Das, the director of Govardhan Ecovillage, and all the residents there for providing the support I needed for this endeavour.

My deep gratitude to Govinda Das, Radha Gopinath Das, Shyamananda Das, Sanat Kumar Das, Srutidharma Das, Pranabandhu Das, Gauranga Das, Siksastakam Das, Vraj Vihari Das and Shubha Vilas Das, who have all been very kind and instrumental in my learning, encouraging me along the way.

Vinay Raniga and Bhavik Patel from London provided much assistance and support right from the conception of the book. Without them this book would have only been a dream and I cannot thank them enough for all that they have done for me.

Thanks to Prem Kishor Das, Chaitanya Rupa Das, Radheshlal Das, Pratik Kapoor, Yashwant Kulkarni, Priyavrat Mafatlal, Sagar Wadekar, Mabick Thapa, Paresh Kochrekar and Shyamgopal Shroff for their ongoing support in my efforts to serve.

Special thanks to everyone who allowed me to share their stories. They brought the messages of the book to life. Particular thanks to Dr Mukund Shanbag, Mrs Pavitra Shanbag, Gandharvika and their family, Mr Snehal Ansariya and Mrs Kiran Ansariya along with their son, Sairaj, and Brigadier Sunil Kumar N.V. for the awe-inspiring stories from the Indian Army, and Hitesh Kotwani.

I am grateful to Satya Gaud and his team for shooting the cover photograph and to Satya Gopinath Das and Chaitanya Tharvala for their help with the graphics.

It was Ms Vaishali Mathur's editorial expertise, along with Ms Udyotna Kumar's efforts, that helped to fine-tune and shape the book the way you see it. Sincere thanks to Ms Rachita Raj and Ms Chanpreet Khurana for their copy-editing and to everyone at Penguin Random House who helped make this happen.

Thanks to the inspiration, encouragement and support of all the ashram and community members of Radha Gopinath Temple, Mumbai, where I live, and the ashram and community members of Bhaktivedanta Manor, London, where I spend the most amount of time outside of India.

Without the selfless love, blessings and support of my loving parents, family, friends and well-wishers, my efforts would be fruitless. Thank you to you all!

Thank you to everyone who follows me online. It is because of every like, comment and share that I got this opportunity to put my thoughts into writing.

Lastly, I offer my sincere thanks to you—all the readers of this book. It is because of you that I have had the opportunity to bring forth my realizations about our journey through life. I hope you enjoy my humble attempt to pass on the wisdom that was given to me by my teachers.

Author's Note

On 9 May 2017, I received a call from Ms Vaishali Mathur, the executive editor and head of rights and language publishing at Penguin Random House India. She had seen a couple of my videos online and wanted to explore the possibility of me writing a book with them. It sounded exciting to me! I had always believed in trying to make a difference in the lives of people by helping them to redefine their thinking. I had been trying to do that through my speaking and lecturing for over two decades, and now here was a golden opportunity to take my purpose to the next level.

Naturally, I wanted to say yes straight away, but there was something within me holding me back. I gave her a typical answer, 'Let's see. I'll get back to you soon,' which, in hindsight, must have been frustrating for her. My reservation came from the fact that I am not a writer. Apart from a couple of articles and poems I had written years ago, the pen was used for signing managerial documents and the keyboard for my diary and records.

A few days later, after the excitement settled and I began to give the offer some serious thought, I received a call from an old friend in London, Sruti Dharma Das. He had been my well-wisher long before my online presence grew. Out of the blue, he was now calling me to remind me that I needed to write a book. 'That is the next step for you,' he said. 'A speaker should have a book to complement his talks, because that will truly benefit his listeners. They can then take your talk home with them! And writing should not be too hard for someone who regularly speaks, anyway.' I felt flattered by his kind words.

A lack of experience in writing wasn't the only issue for me. I travel extensively to speak around the world. I knew that writing a book would need focused time, grounding me in one location to think deeply about what I wanted to offer to the world. However, this would mean cancelling a lot of speaking engagements, letting many people down. It was then, as I scrolled online, that I came across a quote by Sir Richard Branson, 'If someone offers you an amazing opportunity, and you are not sure you can do it, say YES, then learn how to do it later.' That was a sign; I couldn't delay my response any further. I called Ms Mathur to confirm her offer: I was going to try to be an author.

As you will find out from this book, I can wake up in one city and go to sleep in another. Travelling to share my purpose has become a part of who I am. As summer turned to autumn and the monsoons began to settle, the nagging thought of writing the book became stronger. It was in December of that year that I took the month off to meditate and look deeper into the lessons I had learnt throughout my life.

In doing so, many stories and principles I learnt over the years were put on paper. But how to connect them, I wondered. I decided to weave my interactions with so many different individuals together into one story with two characters, Harry and Lalita Iyer. Their modern journey is the journey of many, put into one. Life is a journey. However, if we can learn from the mistakes and best practices of others, we can make our journey worthwhile and joyful. In the course of writing, I realized that it is much harder than giving a talk, but I have also come to terms with the fact that if I can contribute some meaning to the life of another, I am willing to take on the challenge. My only prayer is that this book be blessed by God to bring a positive change in the lives of the readers.